ISBN: 9781697199345

www.thearchitecturequiz.com
@thearchitecturequiz

THE ARCHI- TEC- TURE QUIZ

MIGUEL BOLIVAR

FOREWORD

As a lover of the traditional pub quiz (but often winning the wooden spoon) and all things architecture, I decided to create this book full of architectural trivia. I hope you will have as much fun testing yourself and others as I did creating each quiz.

The Architecture Quiz is aimed at all ages offering a range of difficulties to offer a challenging and educational experience to all readers.

Miguel Bolivar

CONTENTS

001
ARCHITECT QUOTES #1

1. Which American-German architect coined the phrase:
    "Less is more."?

a) Bruno Taut
b) Mies van der Rohe
c) Helmut Jahn
d) Walter Gropius

2. Which Pritzker Architecture Prize-winning architect said:
    "There are 360 degrees, so why stick to one?"

a) Zaha Hadid
b) Toyo Ito
c) Aldo Rossi
d) Frei Otto

3. Which renowned French architect was quoted as saying:
    "Each new situation requires a new architecture"?

a) Manuelle Gautrand
b) Gustav Eiffel
c) Michel Mossessian
d) Jean Nouvel

4. Which famous American architect known for his Modernism said:
    "Architecture is the reaching out for the truth"?

a) Richard Meier
b) Frank Gehry
c) Louis Kahn
d) Thom Mayne

5. Complete the famous Frank Lloyd Wright quote:
    "Study nature, love nature, stay close to nature. ...."

a) It will always save you
b) It will never fail you
c) It will inspire you
d) It will return your love

6. Which Chinese architect and founder of MAD architects stated: "To tell you the truth, I don't mind if people don't understand my work or who I am."?

a) MA Yansong
b) Wang Shu
c) He Jingtang
d) Naihan Li

7. Also known as the 'father of skyscrapers', who said: "Form ever follows function."?

a) Phillip Johnson
b) Louis Sullivan
c) Steven Holl
d) Paul Rudolph

8. Who uttered the famous words: "My architecture is easy to understand and enjoy, I hope it also is hard to forget"?

a) Arthur Casas
b) Rino Levi
c) Gustavo Penna
d) Oscar Niemeyer

9. Which well-known architect and author said: "Life is architecture and architecture is the mirror of life"?

a) Patrick Lau
b) Ken Yiang
c) I.M. Pei
d) Robert Fan

10. Which of these is a famous Mies van der Rohe quote?

a) "Build! Don't Talk."
b) "Even a brick wants to be something."
c) "Architecture is inhabited sculpture."
d) "I call architecture frozen music"

002
ARCHITECTURE IN MOVIES

1. The acclaimed silent film comedian Harold Lloyd supposedly dangles from which building in the film Safety Last! (1923):

a) The Eiffel Tower
b) Westminster Abbey
c) The Empire State Building
d) International Savings Building

2. Where was the chase scene in Skyfall (2012) filmed?

a) The Grand Bazaar, Istanbul, Turkey
b) Old Souk, Byblos, Lebanon
c) Khan El-Khalili Bazaar, Cairo, Egypt
d) Al Balad, Amman, Jordan

3. Which of the following was not featured as a location in the Harry Potter series?

a) Bodleian Library
b) Westminster Tube Station
c) Alnwick Castle
d) Euston Station

4. What is the fictional name of the Fox Plaza, designed by William Pereira, Scott Johnson and Bill Fain, used in the film Die Hard (1988)?

a) Nobokuri Plaza
b) Nakatomi Plaza
c) Nobutara Plaza
d) Manotuku Plaza

5. Which of the following movies didn't use the Bradbury Building (Los Angeles) as a location?

a) Blade Runner (1982)
b) Chinatown (1974)
c) The Artist (2001)
d) La La Land (2016)

6. **Where is the Baumschulenweg Krematorium, featured in Aeon Flux (2005), located?**

a) Berlin
b) Hamburg
c) Frankfurt
d) Cologne

7. **Which skyscraper does the agent Ethan Hunt scale in Mission Impossible 4: Ghost Protocol (2011)?**

a) Shanghai Tower
b) Burj Khalifa
c) One World Trade Center
d) Taipei 101

8. **Which of the following was not used as a location in Inception (2010)?**

a) Port de Bir-Hakeim
b) John Ferraro Building
c) City of Arts and Sciences
d) Gustave Tuck Theatre, UCL

9. **Where do Eggy and his mum live in Kingsman: The Secret Service (2014)?**

a) Balfron Tower
b) Robin Hood Gardens
c) Alexandra & Ainsworth Estate
d) Park Hill

10. **Which of the following does not feature the Eiffel Tower?**

a) Moulin Rouge! (2001)
b) An Education (2009)
c) La Vie En Rose (2007)
d) Midnight in Paris (2011)

003
ARCHITECTURE IN TV SERIES

1. Which brutalist housing building can be seen in the opening credits of the children's classic gameshow Incredible Games (1994-1995)?

a) Trellick Tower
b) The Barbican
c) Balfron Tower
d) Alton Estate

2. Which city doubles for King's Landing in Game of Thrones?

a) Rome
b) Dubrovnik
c) Lagos
d) Valencia

3. What is the original name of Downton Abbey?

a) Blenheim Palace
b) Highclere Castle
c) Chatsworth House
d) Cliveden House

4. Which was used as the Bennet's family house in the BBC limited series Pride and Prejudice?

a) Edgcote House
b) Luckington Court
c) Lyme Park
d) Hatfield House

5. Which of the following characters is an architect?

a) Ted Mosby (How I Met Your Mother)
b) George Costanza (Seinfeld)
c) Claire (Fleabag)
d) Chandler Bing (Friends)

6. **Where does Yasmin Khan, one of the 13th Doctor's companions in Doctor Who, live?**

a) Park Hill
b) Netherthorpe
c) The Fosters
d) Lansdowne Estate

7. **Who designed the Boiler Suit at Guy's Hospital, which can be seen in the series Killing Eve?**

a) Frank Gehry
b) Nicholas Grimshaw
c) David Adjaye
d) Thomas Heatherwick

8. **Where was the correctional facility in Misfits filmed?**

a) The Barbican
b) Finsbury Health Center
c) Thamesmead
d) Mardyke Estate

9. **In the 2016 series Westworld, which architect's 1923 design was used as Jeffrey Wright's character's villa?**

a) Frank Lloyd Wright
b) Louis Sullivan
c) Philip Johnson
d) Daniel Burnham

10. **What's the name of the glass house from the Black Mirror episode 'Smithereens'?**

a) The Cliff House
b) La Casa del Desierto
c) Maison de Rasoir
d) Transparent House

004
POT LUCK

1. Which of these is not an ancient Greek column order?

a) Doric
b) Corinthian
c) Tuscan
d) Ionic

2. What is the architectural element that spans the opening of a door or a window?

a) Lintel
b) Key Stone
c) Arch
d) Bressummer

3. Where is the Parthenon located?

a) Ephesus, Turkey
b) Athens, Greece
c) Rome, Italy
d) Cairo, Egypt

4. Who created the human figure Modulor?

a) Mies van der Rohe
b) Le Corbusier
c) Walter Gropius
d) Frank Lloyd Wright

5. Which of the following are not one of the requirements for architecture according to Vitruvius' principles?

a) Firmitas (Integrity)
b) Utilitas (Utility)
c) Diversitas (Variety)
d) Venustas (Beauty)

6. Which architectural style are the Paris Metro entrance signs designed in?

a) Art Deco
b) Art Nouveau
c) Arts and Crafts
d) Baroque

7. Who was the first female architect to win the Pritzker Architecture Prize?

a) Denise Scott Brown
b) Zaha Hadid
c) Lina Bo Bardi
d) Maya Lin

8. Which of the following is an example of the Postmodern style?

a) No.1 Poultry
b) The National Theatre
c) 30 St Mary Axe (The Gherkin)
d) Lloyd's Building

9. Which of these is not a characteristic of Andrea Palladio's architectural style?

a) Symmetry and proportions
b) Mathematical ratios
c) Geometric forms
d) Undulating lines that mimic nature

10. Who designed the Oslo Opera House?

a) Bjarke Ingels
b) Snøhetta
c) MVDRV
d) Herzog & De Meuron

005
POT LUCK

1. Which architect designed the Louvre Pyramid at the Louvre Museum, Paris?

a) Philip Johnson
b) Frank Lloyd Wright
c) Bjarke Ingels
d) I. M. Pei

2. Who wrote the book Ornament and Crime?

a) Adolf Loos
b) Walter Gropius
c) Le Corbusier
d) Louis Kahn

3. Which of the following is not one of Le Corbusier's five points of architecture?

a) Horizontal Window
b) Pilotis
c) Open Floor Plan
d) White Exterior

4. Who designed the Royal College of Physicians?

a) Berthold Lubetkin
b) Sir Denys Lasdun
c) Auguste Perret
d) Louis Kahn

5. In which style is the SIS Building in London?

a) Brutalist
b) Deconstructivist
c) Postmodernist
d) High-Tech

6. Which of the following is not designed by Sir Christopher Wren?

a) St. Paul's Cathedral
b) Royal Observatory
c) Christchurch Spitalfields
d) Hampton Court

7. What is not a characteristic of Byzantine architecture?

a) High domes
b) Rose windows
c) Elaborate mosaics
d) Use of marble, brick and stone

8. Where in Italy is the Colosseum located?

a) Rome
b) Florence
c) Milan
d) Bologna

9. Who designed the Sydney Opera House?

a) Oscar Niemeyer
b) Arne Jacobsen
c) Jørn Utzon
d) Henning Larsen

10. Which of the following was not built in the Gothic style?

a) Notre-Dame de Paris
b) Salisbury Cathedral
c) Milan Cathedral
d) The Palace of Versailles

006

NORTH AMERICAN ARCHITECTURE

1. Who designed the Empire State Building in New York City?

a) Frank Lloyd Wright
b) William F. Lamb
c) I.M. Pei
d) Mies Van Der Rohe

2. In which year was the Walt Disney Concert Hall in Los Angeles officially opened?

a) 2001
b) 2002
c) 2003
d) 2004

3. In which U.S. state will you find Jim Reed's award-winning Thorncrown Chapel?

a) Arkansas
b) Alabama
c) Texas
d) Nebraska

4. Who did Albert Kahn design the Fisher Building in Detroit for?

a) Lavinia Fisher
b) The Fisher Brothers
c) Carlos Fisher
d) Fisher Incorporated

5. Which building was once referred to as "the most recognizable and beloved building in Los Angeles'?

a) Eastern Columbia Building
b) Hollywood Bowl
c) Stahl House
d) Griffith Observatory

6. Which of these National Historic Landmarks was designed by Charles Alling Gifford?

a) Omni Mount Washington Resort
b) Eads Bridge
c) Hearst Castle
d) Sergeant Floyd Monument

7. Where is the John F. Kennedy Presidential Library and Museum located?

a) Chicago
b) Washington D.C.
c) Boston
d) New York City

8. What is the tallest building in the United States of America?

a) Willis Tower
b) One World Trade Center
c) Aon Center
d) Empire State Building

9. Which famous NYC museum was designed by Frank Lloyd Wright?

a) The Museum of Modern Art
b) The Metropolitan Museum of Art
c) The New York Transit Museum
d) The Guggenheim Museum

10. In which U.S. city would you find the Cathedral of Saint Paul that was designed by Emmanuel Louis Masqueray?

a) St. Paul
b) Duluth
c) Minneapolis
d) St. Cloud

007
AFRICAN ARCHITECTURE

1. Alice Lane Towers, the first South African building to incorporate cutting edge glass technology, can be found in which city?

a) Durban
b) Cape Town
c) Pretoria
d) Johannesburg

2. Who designed the Reunification Monument in Cameroon?

a) Anton Smit
b) Gédéon Mpando
c) Joram Mariga
d) Damian Manuhwa

3. Which African country is home to the largest mosque on the continent?

a) Morocco
b) Mali
c) Algeria
d) Senegal

4. What is the tallest building in South Africa?

a) Carlton Center
b) Ponte Tower
c) The National Reserve Bank
d) The Leonardo

5. The South African Union Buildings were designed by which English Architect?

a) Sir Herbert Baker
b) Christopher Wren
c) Charles Barry
d) Joseph Paxton

6. Which Cape Town landmark is the oldest building in South Africa?

a) Cape Town City Hall
b) The Castle of Good Hope
c) Bertram House
d) Koopmans De Wet House

7. Where can the Great Mosque of Djenné, the largest mud brick building in the world, be found?

a) Egypt
b) Zimbabwe
c) Mali
d) Cameroon

8. Which South African City Hall is considered to be the largest red brick building in the Southern Hemisphere?

a) Pietermaritzburg
b) Kimberly
c) Port Elizabeth
d) Bloemfontein

9. Which African architect co-designed the Smithsonian National Museum of African American History and Culture?

a) Phil Freelon
b) David Ajaye
c) Pacal De Souza
d) Romarick Atoke

10. The Nabembe Tower is a striking skyscraper is which African city?

a) Brazaville
b) Lagos
c) Luanda
d) Nairobi

008
WORLD'S UGLIEST BUILDINGS

1. Completed in 1968, locals wanted which U.S 'brutalist' city hall demolished before it was even completed?

a) Pittsburgh City Hall
b) Baltimore City Hall
c) Denver City Hall
d) Boston City Hall

2. Which building won the 2016 Carbuncle Cup for the ugliest building in the UK?

a) Nova Victoria
b) Lincoln Plaza
c) Cutty Sark London
d) Redrock

3. Who designed the Experience Music Project in Washington which is rated one of the ugliest buildings in the country?

a) Zoltan Pali
b) Marc Appleton
c) Frank Gehry
d) Michael Maltzan

4. Designed by Rafael Viñoly, which building is often called the 'armpit of New York City'?

a) Penn Station
b) 432 Park Avenue
c) The New York Times Building
d) 200 Eleventh Avenue

5. Shaped like a truck, which shopping mall is considered to be the ugliest in Russia?

a) Clover House Shopping Mall
b) Koltso Shopping Mall
c) Fura Shopping Mall
d) Nautilus Shopping Mall

6. **Which building was rated as the second ugliest in the world by CBC Radio?**

a) ZizkovTelevision Tower - Prague
b) Kaden Tower - USA
c) Ryugyong Hotel - North Korea
d) Elephant Building - Bangkok

7. **Shaped like a coin, which of C.Y. Lee's buildings is considered to be one of the ugliest buildings in China?**

a) Taipei 101
b) 85 Sky Tower
c) Farglory Financial Center
d) Fang Yuan Building

8. **While places of worship are typically beautiful, which is considered to be the ugliest church in the world?**

a) Liverpool Metropolitan Cathedral
b) Cardboard Cathedral
c) Crystal Cathedral
d) Brasilia Cathedral

9. **Hardenburg Town Hall is widely considered to be the ugliest building in which European country?**

a) France
b) The Netherlands
c) Belgium
d) Spain

10. **The unsightly Agbar Tower can be found in which prominent European destination?**

a) Madrid
b) Barcelona
c) Paris
d) Lisbon

009
SKYSCRAPERS

1. Who designed the neo-futuristic tower known as Sweden's 'Turning Torso'?

a) Santiago Calatrava
b) Axel Haig
c) Erik Asmussen
d) Peter Celsing

2. What is the Chicago skyscraper formerly known as the Sears Tower now known as?

a) Tower of the Americas
b) Reunion Tower
c) Engelbert Tower
d) Willis Tower

3. Who designed the 310m (1,000ft) tall Shard in London?

a) Frank Lloyd Wright
b) Renzo Piano
c) David Chipperfield
d) James Stirling

4. What is the tallest building in the world?

a) Zifeng Tower
b) One World Trade Center
c) Burj Khalifa
d) Tokyo Skytree

5. In which U.S. city can you find the Transamerica Pyramid?

a) San Francisco
b) Chicago
c) Los Angeles
d) New York City

6. Which three-column skyscraper in Singapore features the biggest rooftop infinity pool in the world?

a) Tanjong Pagar Center
b) Republic Plaza
c) Capital Tower
d) Marina Bay Sands Hotel

7. Which Russian city is home to the country's tallest skyscraper Lakhta Center?

a) Moscow
b) Saint Petersburg
c) Kazan
d) Omsk

8. Which city in Saudi Arabia has a restriction of only 30 usable floors in any building?

a) Riyadh
b) Jeddah
c) Medina
d) Makkah

9. Which famous American skyscraper features in the movie 'King Kong'?

a) Chrysler Building
b) Rockefeller Plaza
c) Empire State Building
d) Central Park Tower

10. Where in Italy would you find the Bosco Verticale, the skyscraper featuring more than 900 trees?

a) Milan
b) Rome
c) Venice
d) Naples

010
BRIDGES

1. What is the name of the first cast-iron bridge, which opened to public use in 1781?

a) Tower Bridge, London
b) The Iron Bridge, Shropshire
c) Pont Au Double, Paris
d) Maria Pia Bridge, Porto

2. Which canceled bridge proposal was to be the latest addition to the River Thames in London and cost the public over £40m?

a) The Pearl Bridge
b) Thames Garden
c) The Garden Bridge
d) The Thames Walkway

3. Where is the longest bridge in the world?

a) Taiwan
b) Kuwait
c) Japan
d) China

4. What is the design style of The Golden Gate Bridge in San Francisco?

a) Postmodernist
b) Art Deco
c) Art Nouveau
d) Modernist

5. Which of the following bridges connects two continents?

a) Bosphorus Bridge, Turkey
b) Guandu Bridge, Taiwan
c) Pont de Brottone, France
d) Danyang–Kunshan Grand Bridge, China

6. Who was the architect of The Millennium Bridge in London?

a) Zaha Hadid
b) Thomas Heatherwick
c) Norman Foster
d) Frank Gehry

7. How high is Tower Bridge in London?

a) 50m (164ft)
b) 17m (56ft)
c) 86m (282ft)
d) 42m (138ft)

8. Which of the following bridges are not located in Venice, Italy?

a) Constitution Bridge
b) Serreria Bridge
c) Bridge of Sighs
d) Rialto Bridge

9. What type of bridge is the George Washington Bridge in New York City?

a) Suspension
b) Truss
c) Arch
d) Cantilever

10. An engineering marvel, which of the following is the tallest bridge in the world?

a) Arrabida Bridge, Portugal
b) Harringworth Viaduct, UK
c) Normandy Bridge, France
d) The Millau Viaduct, France

011
WHO DESIGNED THIS? #1

1. Which Pritzker prize winner designed the Heydar Aliyev Center in Baku, Azerbaijan?

a) Frank Gehry
b) Zaha Hadid
c) Max Cetto
d) Eduardo Souto de Moura

2. Which American art museum was designed by Eero Saarinen, David Kahler, and Santiago Calatrava?

a) Milwaukee Art Museum
b) Los Angeles County Museum of Art
c) Art Institute of Chicago
d) National Gallery of Art

3. Who designed the White House in Washington D.C?

a) Michale Graves
b) James Hoban
c) Cass Gilbert
d) Daniel Libeskind

4. Who designed the Seattle Space Needle that was built in 1962 for the World's Fair?

a) Frank Gehry & Edward E. Carlson
b) John Graham & Frank Lloyd Wright
c) Edward E. Carlson & John Graham
d) Phillip Johnson & Robert Fan

5. Who designed the Burj Al Arab in Dubai?

a) Tom Wright
b) Enrique Norten
c) Rem Koolhaas
d) Richard Rogers

6. Who designed the iconic Tower Bridge in London?

a) Christopher Wren
b) Charles Barry
c) James Wyatt
d) Sir Horace Jones

7. Which architect designed Casa Milà, also known as the 'stone quarry' in Spain?

a) Pere Blai
b) Antoni Gaudi
c) Josep Maria Jujol
d) Josep Casals

8. Located in New Delhi, the Lotus Temple was designed by which architect?

a) Hossein Amanat
b) Bahram Shirdel
c) Ahmad Jafari
d) Fariborz Sahba

9. Who designed the iconic Leaning Tower of Pisa in Italy?

a) Bonanno Pisano
b) Carlo Mademo
c) Pietro da Cortona
d) Ferdinando Fuga

10. Which architect was responsible for the magnificent design of the Chrysler Building in NYC?

a) Mies van der Rohe
b) Robert Venturi
c) William Van Alen
d) Steven Holl

012
CASTLES

1. Who was the Neuschwanstein Castle in Germany built for?

a) King Ludwig II
b) King Rupert
c) Frederick The Great
d) King William I

2. Which castle near Normandy, France is considered to be one of architecture's greatest achievements?

a) Château de Chenonceau
b) Mont Saint Michel
c) Château de Cheverny
d) Peyrepertuse

3. Which castle has the reputation of being the most haunted one in Scotland?

a) Balmoral Castle
b) Stirling Castle
c) Glamis Castle
d) Spynie Palace

4. Who built Kilkenny Castle in Ireland in 1195?

a) Bill Morcom
b) William Herbert
c) Jasper Tudor
d) William Marshal

5. Which Belgian castle is also known as the Noisy Castle?

a) Gravensteen Castle
b) Miranda Castle
c) Gaasbeek Castle
d) Alden biesen Castle

6. **Which castle is the official residence of the British royal family in Berkshire?**

a) Windsor Castle
b) Warwick Castle
c) Leeds Castle
d) Dover Castle

7. **In which country will you find the only royal castle in the Western hemisphere?**

a) Cuba
b) Venezuela
c) Mexico
d) Peru

8. **Which Slovenian castle is built in a cave underneath a natural rock arch?**

a) Little Castle
b) Bogensperk Castle
c) Bled Castle
d) Predjama Castle

9. **In which country will you find Bran Castle which is often considered to be linked to Count Dracula?**

a) Romania
b) Belarus
c) Moldova
d) Russia

10. **Which castle was named a UNESCO World Heritage Site in 1981?**

a) Château Usse
b) Château Blois
c) Château Rivau
d) Château de Chambord

013
PRITZKER PRIZE WINNERS

1. Which Mexican architect won the Pritzker prize in 1980?

a) Mario Pani
b) Louis Barragan
c) Enrique Norten
d) Max Cetto

2. The 2017 Pritzker prize winners - a team of three consisting of Rafael Aranda, Carme Pigem, and Ramon Vilalta - hail from where?

a) Portugal
b) Argentina
c) Spain
d) Brazil

3. German architect Frei Otto won the Pritzker prize in which year?

a) 2015
b) 2013
c) 2010
d) 2008

4. Known for transparent, high-tech designs, who won the Pritzker prize in 2007?

a) Zaha Hadid
b) Jean Nouvel
c) Toyo Ito
d) Richard Rogers

5. Best known for designing the Sydney Opera House, which architect won the Pritzker prize in 2003?

a) Frank Gehry
b) Jørn Utzon
c) Aldo Rossi
d) Wang Shu

6. **Balkrishna Doshi, the 2018 winner, is the first Pritzker Laureate from which country?**

a) Bangladesh
b) Pakistan
c) India
d) Sri Lanka

7. **In which year did American architect Robert Venturi win the Pritzker prize?**

a) 1991
b) 1993
c) 1996
d) 1998

8. **Who was awarded the first-ever Pritzker Architecture Prize in 1979?**

a) Sverre Fehn
b) Kenzo Tange
c) Richard Meier
d) Philip Johnson

9. **The 2011 winner Eduardo Souto de Moura hails from which country?**

a) Sweden
b) Portugal
c) Italy
d) Mexico

10. **Known for his innovative use of glass, who won the Pritzker prize in 1982?**

a) Hans Hollein
b) Thom Mayne
c) Kevin Roche
d) Peter Zumthor

014
WHAT IS TALLER?

1. Which of these towers in the U.S is the tallest?

a) Willis Tower
b) Trump International Hotel & Tower
c) Bank of America Tower
d) Salesforce Tower

2. Which of these famous world monuments is the tallest?

a) San Jacinto Monument, Texas
b) Washington Monument, Washinton D.C.
c) Victory Monument, Russia
d) Gateway Arch, Missouri

3. Which of these skyscrapers is the tallest?

a) Taipei 101
b) Lotte World Tower
c) China Zun
d) CTF Finance Center

4. Which statue is currently the tallest in the world?

a) The Guanyin of Nanshan
b) The Statue of Liberty
c) The Ushiku Great Buddha
d) The Statue of Unity

5. What is the tallest building in Australia?

a) Eureka Tower
b) Q1
c) Rialto Towers
d) 120 Collins Street

6. Which is the tallest all-residential building in the world?

a)   The Torch, Dubai
b)   Burj Mohammed, Abu Dhabi
c)   432 Park Avenue, NYC
d)   220 Central Park South, NYC

7. Which of these is the tallest building in Canada?

a)   Commerce Court West
b)   First Canadian Place
c)   Scotia Plaza
d)   Number One Bloor

8. Which of these buildings in China towers above the rest?

a)   Shangai Tower
b)   Goldin Finance 117
c)   Canton Tower
d)   China Zun Tower

9. Which building in London is the tallest?

a)   Heron Tower
b)   One Canada Square
c)   Citigroup Center
d)   The Shard

10. Which of these popular buildings is the tallest in Germany?

a)   Main Tower
b)   Silver Tower
c)   Commerzbank Tower
d)   Post Tower

015
ANCIENT ARCHITECTURE #1

1. Which is considered to be the oldest pyramid in Egypt dating back to 2630 B.C?

a) Pyramid of Khufu
b) Pyramid of Djoser
c) Pyramid of Menkaure
d) Pyramid of Teti

2. Which nickname was given to the ancient crypt Al Khazneh that was constructed out of rose-coloured sandstone?

a) Treasury at Petra
b) The Jordan Vault
c) The Khazneh Treasury
d) The Pharaoh's Lair

3. Where in the world will you find the 11 Megalithic Temples ?

a) Greece
b) Tunisia
c) Malta
d) Turkey

4. Most commonly known as the Temple of Athena, which ancient structure has served as both a Christian church and a fortress?

a) Propylaea
b) Bassae
c) Temple of Apollo
d) The Parthenon

5. Which ancient Roman structure was commissioned by Julius Caesar and became the template for many buildings to follow?

a) Circus Maximus
b) Theatre of Marcellus
c) Trajan Forum
d) Stadium of Domitian

6. The Sanchi Stupa is one of the oldest stone structures in which country?

a) India
b) Vietnam
c) Afghanistan
d) Burma

7. Built using 30 million shelly limestones, what ancient three-tier aqueduct spans the Gardon River in Southern France?

a) Aqua Paola
b) Pont du Paris
c) Pont Du Gard
d) Aqua Felice

8. Borobudur, the largest Buddhist temple in the world, is situated in which Indonesian Province?

a) South Sumatra
b) West Java
c) Riau
d) Central Java

9. Which marble masterpiece and iconic symbol of love was recognised as a World Heritage Site by UNESCO in 1983?

a) The Marble Palace
b) The Taj Mahal
c) The Washington Monument
d) Sheikh Zayed Mosque

10. Which famous Turkish fortress was under construction for over a century before finally being completed in 1,000 B.C?

a) Van Fortress
b) Rumeli Fortress
c) Anadolu Fortress
d) Payas Fortress

016
LANDMARKS

1. Which famous American landmark was a gift from France to commemorate the alliance between countries during the revolution?

a) The Gateway Arch
b) The Statue of Liberty
c) Golden Gate Bridge
d) The Belle of Louisville

2. The Machu Picchu Archaeological Park is perched on a mountaintop in which mountain range?

a) Andes Mountains
b) Himalayas
c) Atlas Mountains
d) Ural Mountains

3. How long is the Great Wall of China, the longest wall in the world?

a) 11,830 miles
b) 18,220 miles
c) 9,340 miles
d) 13,170 miles

4. Construction started on which imposing Spanish building in 1982 and is only set to be completed in 2026 after 144 years?

a) Plaza De Toros de Las Ventas
b) Palacio Real
c) La Sagrada Familia
d) Alhambra

5. The Christ the Redeemer Statue keeps a watchful eye over the people of which South American city?

a) Manaus
b) Rio de Janeiro
c) Lima
d) Bogota

6. Which Russian landmark boasts more than 20 towers, 4 churches, and 5 palaces within its walls?

a) The Kremlin
b) Red Square
c) Kizhi Island
d) Mayakovskaya

7. Who designed one of South Africa's most renowned landmarks, the Afrikaans Language Monument?

a) Herman Manneeldt
b) Peet Haasbroek
c) Kurt Koppel
d) Jan van Wijk

8. What is the name of the colossal mosque in Abu Dhabi that can accommodate more than 40,000 worshippers?

a) Al Aziz Mosque
b) ADNOC Mosque
c) Sheikh Zayed Grand Mosque
d) Bani Hashim Mosque

9. In which popular Bangkok landmark does the famous green jade statue of Buddha reside?

a) The Imperial Palace
b) The Grand Palace
c) The Royal Palace
d) The Regal Palace

10. Who designed the Petronas Twin Towers, a popular landmark in Kuala Lumpur, Malaysia?

a) Cesar Pelli
b) Jon Mitsui
c) Norman Foster
d) Aldo Rossi

017
ANCIENT WONDERS

1. Which famous Roman amphitheatre was completed in 80 A.D, with a seating capacity of over 50,000?

a) The Colosseum
b) Amphitheatre at Epidaurus
c) Arles Amphitheatre
d) Leptis Magna Arena

2. How many stone blocks were used in the construction of the Great Pyramid of Giza?

a) 3.9 million
b) 2.3 million
c) 1.8 million
d) 5 million

3. In which European city can the Baths of Trajan be found?

a) Athens
b) Barcelona
c) Rome
d) Venice

4. Which ancient Mausoleum was designed by Greek architects and four sculptors - one for each side of the structure?

a) Taj Mahal
b) Shah-i-Zinda
c) Mausoleum of the Shirvanshahs
d) Mausoleum at Halicarnassus

5. Which Egyptian lighthouse was one of the tallest structures in the world up until 1300 B.C?

a) Lighthouse of Alexandria
b) Tour de Cordouan
c) Kōpu Lighthouse
d) Tower of Hercules

6. What is the Sultan Ahmed Mosque in Istanbul, Turkey also known as?

a) The Red Mosque
b) The Blue Mosque
c) The Yellow Mosque
d) The Green Mosque

7. Saksaywaman is a walled Inca fortress located in which country?

a) Bolivia
b) Ecuador
c) Peru
d) Venezuela

8. What nickname was given to Chand Baori, the stepweel situated in the village of Abhaneri in India?

a) The City of Brightness
b) The Sleeping City
c) The City with Stairs
d) The Traveling City

9. In which county of the United Kingdom would you find the architectural marvel known as Stonehenge?

a) Surrey
b) Berkshire
c) Hampshire
d) Wiltshire

10. In which year did construction on the Leaning Tower of Pisa, Italy commence?

a) 1278
b) 1173
c) 1069
d) 1355

018
CATHEDRALS

1. Which world-renowned cathedral was destroyed in a fire in 2019?

a) Nidaros Cathedral
b) Notre Dame Cathedral
c) León Cathedral
d) St Charles Cathedral

2. At which London cathedral did Prince Charles and Lady Diana Spencer get married?

a) St Paul's Cathedral
b) Southwark Cathedral
c) Westminster Abbey
d) St George's Cathedral

3. Which cathedral is the tallest in the world?

a) Freiburg Cathedral
b) Strasbourg Cathedral
c) Cologne Cathedral
d) Ulm Minster

4. Who designed the spectacular St Paul's Cathedral in London?

a) Richard Rogers
b) Christopher Wren
c) Herbert Baker
d) John Soane

5. What is the largest cathedral in the world?

a) Liverpool Cathedral, UK
b) Cathedral of Saint John The Divine, U.S
c) Milan Cathedral, Italy
d) Cathedral of Our Lady, Belgium

6. By which name is the Cathedral of the Intercession of the Most Holy Theotokos on the Moat more commonly know?

a) St Basil's Cathedral
b) St Isaac's Cathedral
c) Ascension Cathedral
d) Dormition Cathedral

7. The tomb of Christopher Columbus is located just outside the entrance to which cathedral?

a) The Cathedral of Saint Sava, Serbia
b) Uspenski Cathedral, Finland
c) Holy Trinity Cathedral of Tbilisi, Georgia
d) Seville Cathedral, Spain

8. Which cathedral serves as the headquarters of the archbishop of the Roman Catholic Archdiocese of New York?

a) Washington National Cathedral
b) The Cathedral of St. Patrick
c) Grace Cathedral
d) Trinity Cathedral

9. Which cathedral was left unfinished for 350 years, taking nearly 600 years in total to be completed in 880?

a) Amiens Cathedral
b) The Chartes Cathedral
c) Cologne Cathedral
d) Frankfurt Cathedral

10. Which cathedral is widely recognized as the finest example English Gothic Architecture?

a) Salisbury Cathedral
b) St Stephen's Cathedral
c) Zagreb Cathedral
d) St Sophia Cathedral

019
STIRLING PRIZE WINNERS

1. Wilkinson Eyre Architects won the 2002 Stirling Prize for which structure?

a) Ernsting's Service Center
b) Gateshead Millennium Bridge
c) Hampden Gurney Primary School
d) National Gallery of Ireland

2. Who designed the 2007 winning building, the Museum of Modern Literature in Germany?

a) Glenn Howells Architects
b) Haworth Tompkins
c) David Chipperfield Architects
d) Foster and Partners

3. The Evelyn Theatre in Liverpool won the Stirling Prize in which year?

a) 2014
b) 2009
c) 2017
d) 2015

4. Who was the winning architect of the Stirling Prize in both 2010 and 2011?

a) David Adjaye
b) Eric Parry
c) Peter Cook
d) Zaha Hadid

5. How many times has Foster + Partners won the Stirling Prize?

a) Once
b) Twice
c) Three times
d) Five times

6. **What makes the 2019 Stirling Prize winner different from all previous nominees and winners?**

a) First council houses to be short-listed
b) A public vote secured the win
c) The winning building is not in the EU
d) The win was publicly contested

7. **Who is the RIBA Stirling Prize named after?**

a) Peter Stirling
b) James Stirling
c) Anthony Stirling
d) Edward Stirling

8. **Which museum by Foster + Partners won the award in 1998?**

a) Museum of Liverpool
b) Tate Modern
c) Horniman Museum
d) Imperial War Museum

9. **Terminal 4 of which airport won the coveted award in 2006?**

a) Orly Airport, France
b) Dortmund Airport, Germany
c) Barajas Airport, Spain
d) Malpensa Airport, Italy

10. **Which David Chipperfield Architects' design won the Stirling Prize in 2007?**

a) Museum of Modern Literature
b) Museum Island
c) Neues Museum
d) Lenbachhaus

020
POT LUCK

1. Architect John Lloyd-Wright, son of Frank, was the inventor of which popular U.S kids' toy?

a) Duplo Blocks
b) Lincoln Logs
c) Kaleido Gears
d) K'Nex

2. How many bricks were reportedly used to build the Empire State Building, New York?

a) 10 million
b) 5 million
c) 15 million
d) 20 million

3. Who designed the Big Ben tower at the Houses of Parliament in London?

a) John Soane
b) Augustus Pugin
c) Nigel Coates
d) Lewis Cubitt

4. Who is the presenter of the TV show 'The World's Most Extraordinary Homes'?

a) Kevin McCloud
b) John Wisbarth
c) Piers Taylor
d) Dan Jones

5. Who designed the National Women's Monument in South Africa?

a) Revel Fox
b) Joe Noero
c) James Cope Christie
d) Frans Soff

6. Which is the biggest shopping mall in the world?

a) New South China Mall, China
b) Golden Resources Mall, China
c) SM Megamall, Philippines
d) 1 Utama, Malaysia

7. Who designed the Sistine Chapel in Rome?

a) Baccio Pontelli
b) Michelangelo
c) Giovanni dei Dolci
d) Pietro Perugino

8. Where can you find the Living Water Wayside Chapel - the smallest chapel in the world?

a) Liverpool, UK
b) Ontario, Canada
c) Cape Town, South Africa
d) Las Vegas, Nevada

9. In which year did Ryue Nishizawa (age 44) become the youngest winner of the Pritzker Architecture Prize?

a) 2019
b) 2000
c) 2010
d) 1996

10. How old was Frank Lloyd Wright when he died?

a) 91
b) 87
c) 63
d) 71

021
MILITARY ARCHITECTURE

1. Which Russian architect designed the main building of the Russian Ministry of Defense?

a) Lev Rudnev
b) Ivan Fomin
c) Vladimir Shukhov
d) Ivan Rerberg

2. In which U.S. State can you find the United States Army Aviation Museum?

a) Nevada
b) Kentucky
c) Alabama
d) Delaware

3. What is the name of the largest military monument in Europe, located in Leipzig, Germany?

a) Monument to the Battle of Nations
b) Monument of World War II
c) The Remembrance Monument
d) Monument of the Fallen Soldiers

4. What is the home of the U.S. Department of Defense known as?

a) The Hectagon
b) The Pentagon
c) The Polygon
d) The Octagon

5. Which U.S one million square foot spy center storage facility was opened at the start of 2013?

a) The Benning Center
b) Fort Hood
c) Area 51
d) Utah Data Center

6. What name was given to the island forts off the coast of England that served as defence stations during World War I?

a) Rutherford Forts
b) Cape May Bunker
c) Fort Terry
d) Palmerston Forts

7. Which military base features a range of connected underground tunnels that were once used by the Russians as a weapon plant?

a) Taymyr Island Base
b) Herald Island Base
c) Sazan Island Base
d) Yaya Island Base

8. Which island fortress was constructed in the Florida Keys in 1846 to help fight against Caribbean pirates?

a) Fort Jefferson
b) Fort Bailey
c) Fort Rudling
d) Fort Wentworth

9. What is the largest active duty army base in the U.S?

a) Lewis-McCord Base
b) Fort Campbell
c) Fort Hood
d) Fort Benning

10. How big is the Pentagon?

a) 1.9 million square feet
b) 4.5 million square feet
c) 6.6 million square feet
d) 7.3 million square feet

022
SUSTAINABLE ARCHITECTURE

1. Which Manchester, UK building was awarded an "Outstanding" BREEAM rating for sustainability?

a) One Angel Square
b) Five Hallow Avenue
c) Twenty - Two on Main
d) One Dempsy Square

2. Which popular skyscraper has wind turbines located near the top to power the external lighting as well as the parking areas?

a) Burj Khalifa
b) Shanghai Tower
c) One Wolrd Trade Center
d) Zifeng Tower

3. Which was the first skyscraper to receive Leadership in Energy and Environmental Design (LEED) Platinum certification?

a) New York Times Building
b) Rockefeller Plaza
c) One Bryant Park
d) 40 Wall Street

4. Which commercial building is considered to be the greenest in the world?

a) Columbia Center, Washington
b) Hilltop Plaza, Texas
c) The Crown Center, Ohio
d) The Bullitt Center, Washington

5. Ecomo Homes have been designed using only sustainable design principles in which country?

a) South Africa
b) Tanzania
c) Lesotho
d) Swaziland

6. What does the Sun-Moon Mansion in Dezhou, China resemble?

a) A crescent moon
b) A sundial
c) The sun
d) A coin

7. Which architect designed Canada's Manitoba Hydro Place?

a) Dan Hanganu
b) Jack Diamond
c) Bruce Kuwabara
d) Mosh Safdie

8. Which tower that is one of the UK's tallest, was fitted with more than $8 million worth of solar panels to bring it into the 21st century?

a) City Tower
b) Beetham Tower
c) Student Castle
d) CIS Tower

9. How many wind towers does the Bahrain World Trade Center have sandwiched between its two towers?

a) Three
b) Two
c) One
d) Five

10. Which tsunami-proof, sustainable building in China is reportedly as long as the Empire State Building is Tall?

a) KK100
b) Vanke Center
c) China Zun
d) CITIC Plaza

023
ARCHITECTS

1. Who was Frank Lloyd Wright's first employee and also one of the earliest licensed female architects in the world?

a) Maya Lin
b) Marion Mahony Griffin
c) Neri Oxman
d) Sharon Davis

2. Elisabeth Scott became the first female to win an international architectural competition for her design of what?

a) Shakespeare Memorial Theatre
b) The Rose Theatre
c) The George Inn
d) Playhouse Yard

3. Who designed the São Paulo Museum of Art?

a) Gae Aulenti
b) Franca Helg
c) Lina Bo Bardi
d) Lella Vignelli

4. Who was the first black woman to be licensed as an architect both in California and New York?

a) Beverly Greene
b) Ethel Furman
c) Mabel Wilson
d) Norma Merrick Sklarek

5. At what educational institution did Zaha Hadid study mathematics before studying architecture?

a) Canadian University Dubai
b) Yasar University
c) American University of Beirut
d) Qatar University

6. Which renowned architect is also the Dean at Columbia University's Graduate School of Architecture, Planning, and Preservation?

a) Jeanne Gang
b) Amale Andraos
c) Deborah Burke
d) Susana Torre

7. Which American-Israeli designer and architect is well known for her environmental design and digital morphogenesis?

a) Neri Oxman
b) Ada Karmi-Melamede
c) Dora Gad
d) Lotte Cohn

8. Who designed the Vietnam Veterans Memorial in Washington, D.C?

a) Amanda Levete
b) Elizabeth Diller
c) Annabelle Selldorf
d) Maya Lin

9. Which renowned British female architect was involved in the building of the Royal Institute of British Architecture?

a) Edith Hughes
b) Dame Jane Drew
c) Norah Aiton
d) Mary Medd

10. Who was dubbed the UK's first female architect and was also known to tutor Sir Christopher Wren on occasion?

a) Lady Elizabeth Wilbraham
b) Dora Gordine
c) Patty Hopkins
d) Alison Smithson

024
ARCHITECTURE IN MOVIES #2

1. Which Skylab Architecture project doubled as the Cullen family home in Twilight (2008)?

a) Columbia Building
b) Hoke House
c) Skyline Residence
d) Sinbin

2. The Phaeno Science Center by Zaha Hadid doubled as a secret lair in which popular film?

a) The Bank Job (2008)
b) The Transporter (2002)
c) The International (2009)
d) Spy Kids (2001)

3. Which popular USA landmark features in Transformers: Dark of the Moon (2011), Mars Attacks! (1996), and G.I. Joe: Retaliation (2013)?

a) The White House
b) Statue of Liberty
c) Mount Rushmore
d) Empire State Building

4. Which famous landmark was torn apart by a gigantic construction robot in Transformers: Revenge Of The Fallen (2009)?

a) The Eiffel Tower
b) The Leaning Tower of Pisa
c) Sydney Opera House
d) Great Pyramid of Giza

5. Which X-Men character obliterated the Golden Gate Bridge in X-Men: The Last Stand (2013) ?

a) Wolverine
b) Magneto
c) Professor X
d) Cyclops

6. Where is the real-life location of the Tributes' Quarters and Training Center in The Hunger Games: Catching Fire (2013)?

a) Marriott Courtyard, Niagara Falls
b) Marriott Hotel, New Orleans
c) Marriott Marquis Hotel, Atlanta
d) Marriott Marquis Hotel, NYC

7. The Last House on the Left (2009) was partially filmed at which Cape Town attraction?

a) The Helderberg Nature Reserve
b) V&A Waterfront
c) The Castle
d) University of Cape Town

8. In which of these movies does the Empire State Building not feature?

a) Sleepless in Seattle (1993)
b) Isn't It Romantic (2019)
c) Independence Day (1994)
d) Elf (2004)

9. John Lautner's Schaffer House featured in which movie starring Colin Firth and Julianne Moore?

a) Gambit (2012)
b) Bridget Jones's Diary (2001)
c) Pride and Prejudice (1995)
d) A Single Man (2009)

10. Which famous NYC hotel has featured in movies such as Maid in Manhattan (2002), Coming to America (1988), and Scent of a Woman (1992)?

a) Q4 Hotel
b) Crowne Plaza Times Square
c) Waldorf Astoria
d) The Roosevelt Hotel

025
ARCHITECTURE IN TV SERIES #2

1. Scenes for which popular medical series were filmed at the Veterans Administration Sepulveda Ambulatory Care Center in California?

a) The Good Doctor
b) Grey's Anatomy
c) Chicago Med
d) The Resident

2. Which Los Angeles home has become better known as the haunted mansion from American Horror Story?

a) Alfred F. Rosenheim Mansion
b) Greystone Mansion
c) Playboy Mansion
d) Hearst Mansion

3. In which of these TV series did the iconic Manchester Town Hall feature?

a) Line of Duty
b) Foyle's War
c) Vera
d) Shetland

4. Olivia Pope's office building in Scandal is actually which popular Los Angeles attraction?

a) Palace Theatre
b) Ahmanson Theatre
c) The Tower Theatre
d) El Rey Theatre

5. Where can you find the real 'Cheers' bar - the same one that was featured in the popular TV series of the eighties?

a) Englewod, Chicago
b) Inman Park, Atlanta
c) Beacon Hill, Boston
d) Eastport, Annapolis

6. The exterior of which Frank Lloyd Wright building featured extensively in the cult-classic Buffy the Vampire Slayer?

a) The Guggenheim Museum
b) Ennis House
c) Marin County Civic Center
d) Taliesin

7. In which New York building is the U.S version of The Apprentice filmed?

a) Empire State Building
b) Trump Tower
c) Chrysler Building
d) Rockefeller Plaza

8. Which real-life penitentiary was the inspiration behind the Federal Penitentiary of Sona in the Prison Break TV series?

a) Penas Ciudad Barrios Prison
b) Wilkinson Prison
c) San Pedro Prison
d) Carandiru Penitentiary

9. Where in London do Betty and Daniel run into each other in the series finale of Ugly Betty?

a) Trafalgar Square
b) Houses of Parliament
c) Piccadilly Circus
d) Westminster Abbey

10. Which TV show is regularly shot on location outside the Rockerfeller Center?

a) Will & Grace
b) Big Bang Theory
c) 30 Rock
d) Modern Family

026
ARCHITECT QUOTES #2

1. Who said:
   "Architecture is a dangerous mix of power and importance."?

a) Albert Aalbers
b) Rem Koolhaas
c) Pieter Post
d) Thomas Karsten

2. Which renowned architect said:
   "To create, one must first question everything."?

a) Eileen Grey
b) Zaha Hadid
c) Norah Aiton
d) Mary Medd

3. Who said
   "The Sun does not realise how wonderful it is until after a room is made."?

a) John Calvin Stevens
b) Peter Eisenman
c) Cass Gilbert
d) Louis Kahn

4. Best known for his 'Glass House', who said:
   "Architecture is the art of how to waste space."?

a) Steven Johnson
b) Frank Gehry
c) Philip Johnson
d) Bruce Jameson

5. Renzo Piano stated:
   "Architects spend an entire life with this unreasonable idea that you can fight against ...."?

a) Failure
b) Gravity
c) Technology
d) The elements

Answers to 025

1. b) Grey's Anatomy	4. a) Palace Theatre	8. d) Carandiru Penitentiary
2. a) Alfred F. Rosenheim Mansion	5. c) Beacon Hill, Boston	9. a) Trafalgar Square
3. b) Foyle's War	6. b) Ennis House	10. c) 30 Rock
	7. b) Big Brother	

6. Who said:
    "Great buildings that move the spirit have always been rare. In every case they are unique, poetic, products of the heart."?
a) Arthur Erickson
b) George Baird
c) Bing Thom
d) David Ewart

7. From which country is Arne Jacobsen, the architect who said: "If a building becomes architecture, then it is art"?

a) Sweden
b) Germany
c) Finland
d) Denmark

8. Who said:
    "I try to give people a different way of looking at their surroundings. That's art to me."?
a) Maya Lin
b) Elizabeth Diller
c) Beverly Willis
d) Deborah Berke

9. Who said:
    "The straight line belongs to man, the curved line belongs to God."?

a) Pere Blai
b) Jeroni Martorell i Terrats
c) Antonio Gaudi
d) Oscar Tusquets

10. Which award-winning architect said:
    "I don't know why people hire architects and then tell them what to do."?
a) Herbert Baker
b) Frank Gehry
c) Anton Smit
d) Bruno Taut

027
WHO DESIGNED THIS? #2

1. Who designed the Thalian Hall in Wilmington, North Carolina?

a) Thomas W. Lamb
b) John Eberson
c) John Montague Trimble
d) S. Charles Lee

2. The Metropol Parasol in Seville, Spain was designed by which German architect?

a) Jürgen Mayer
b) Peter Behrens
c) Leo von Klenze
d) Albert Speer

3. Which Pritzker-Prize winning architect was credited with designing the Perot Museum of Nature and Science in Dallas?

a) Peter Eisenham
b) Thom Mayne
c) I.M. Pei
d) Julia Morgan

4. Who designed the Guangzhou Opera House in China?

a) Jean Nouvel
b) Toyo Ito
c) Aldo Rossi
d) Zaha Hadid

5. Who designed 30 St Mary Axe (also known as 'The Gherkin') in London?

a) Frank Lloyd Wright
b) Ludwig Mies van der Rohe
c) Norman Foster
d) Ken Shuttleworth

6. **Frank Lloyd Wright designed the Guggenheim in NYC but who designed the Guggenheim Bilbao in Spain?**

a) Frank Gehry
b) Richard Rogers
c) Eero Saarinen
d) Antoni Gaudi

7. **Absolute World in Ontario was designed by MAD Architects, a practice founded by which esteemed architect?**

a) Zhang Ke
b) Ma Yansong
c) Ai Weiwei
d) He Jingtang

8. **The ground-breaking Flatiron Building, NYC was designed by who?**

a) Erik Larson
b) Frederick Law Olmsted
c) Daniel Burnham
d) Dankmar Adler

9. **Who designed the spectacular Zeitz Museum of Contemporary Art Africa that is situated at the V&A waterfront in Cape Town?**

a) Thomas Heatherwick
b) David Chipperfield
c) Glen Howells
d) Jane Duncan

10. **The Tianjin Binhai New Area Library in China, nicknamed The Eye, was designed by which group of architects?**

a) Wilkinson Eyre Architects
b) Future Systems
c) Foster & Partners
d) MVRDV Architects

028
ARCHITECT'S STATIONARY

1. What is commonly used to keep an architect's drawings safe during transportation and storage?

a) Lever-arch file
b) Storage tube
c) Briefcase
d) Folder

2. What is the top layer of a self healing cutting mat made typically made from?

a) Plastic
b) Vinyl
c) Cork
d) Rubber

3. What would an architect use a drafting brush for?

a) To keep drawings clean
b) To sweep the floor with
c) To clean work surfaces
d) To clean a computer keyboard with

4. What is widely considered to be an architect's best friend?

a) Ream of paper
b) Laser Pointer
c) Camera
d) A new pen

5. Which of these types of paper is commonly used by an architect?

a) Sugar Paper
b) Tissue Paper
c) Tracing paper
d) Duplicate paper

6. Why is a red pen so important to an architect?

a) It is used to indicate danger areas
b) It is used for redlining
c) It is use to indicate entrances and exits
d) It looks nicer than a black or blue pen

7. Which simple tool allows an architect to measure accurately using the imperial or metric scale?

a) Scale ruler
b) Measuring tape
c) Yard stick
d) Calipers

8. Who invented the drafting machine back in 1901?

a) Matthias Theel
b) Charles Henry Gould
c) John J Loud
d) Charles H. Little

9. Which tool is used for cutting edges at an angle when building a model?

a) Mitre Box
b) Scissors
c) Scalpel
d) Edger

10. Who patented the protracting trigonometer in 1858?

a) Thomas Edison
b) Granville Woods
c) Josiah Lyman
d) Benjamin Bradley

029
POT LUCK

1. At which university did Frank Lloyd Wright study?

a) University of Wisconsin
b) UCLA
c) Duke University
d) Columbia University

2. Which popular monthly magazine was launched as a California trade quarterly in 1920?

a) Landscape Architecture Magazine
b) The Architect's Diary
c) Architectural Digest
d) Volume Zero

3. Who narrated the 1998 historical documentary entitled 'Frank Lloyd Wright'

a) Kelsey Grammer
b) Alan Alda
c) Steve Buscemi
d) Edward Herrmann

4. Which of these is a popular design software for architects?

a) SketchUp
b) Gimp
c) Outlook
d) Ableton Live

5. Who designed the Beehive in Wellington, New Zealand?

a) Miles Warren
b) Basil Spence
c) Pete Bossley
d) Ron Sang

6. What is the oldest University still in operation in the world?

a) Oxford University, UK
b) University of Salamanca, Spain
c) University of Karueein, Morocco
d) University of Padua, Italy

7. With a capacity of 114,000, what is the largest sport stadium in the world?

a) Michigan Stadium
b) Ohio Stadium
c) Kyle Field
d) Rungrado May Day Stadium

8. Who wrote the beautifully-illustrated Architecture: Form, Space, and Order?

a) Kenneth Brian Frampton
b) Rem Koolhaas
c) Frank Ching
d) Frank Lloyd Wright

9. What is the most-photographed building in the world?

a) The Eiffel Tower
b) The Burj Khalifa
c) Empire State Building
d) Big Ben

10. What is the largest art museum in the world?

a) Metropolitan Museum of Art, NYC
b) The Louvre, Paris
c) Victoria and Albert Museum, London
d) Museum of Fine Arts, Vienna

030
ARCHITECTURAL STYLES

1. Which of these is not a prime example of Baroque architecture?

a) Buckingham Palace
b) Palace of Versailles
c) Les Invalides
d) St. Peter's Square

2. Thatched roofs, casement windows, and masonry chimneys are all common features of which architectural style?

a) Victorian
b) Modernism
c) Tudor
d) Islamic

3. The Notre Dame Cathedral in Paris is an example of which architectural style?

a) Neo-classical
b) Gothic
c) Romanesque
d) Victorian

4. What type of architecture can include styles such as Futurism, Post-modern and New Classical?

a) Vernacular architecture
b) Classical architecture
c) Art Deco
d) Modernism

5. The 1988 MoMA exhibition celebrating which architectural style brought together the likes of Zaha Hadid, Frank Gehry, and Wolf Prix?

a) Deconstructivism
b) Art Nouveau
c) Beaux-Arts
d) Gothic revival

6. Which of these buildings cannot be classified as Romanesque architecture?

a) Church of St. Trophime
b) Bamberg Cathedral
c) St Paul's Cathedral
d) Modena Cathedral

7. Which of these people did not contribute to the Renaissance design of the St Peter's Basilica in the Vatican City?

a) Donato Bramante
b) Carlo Maderno
c) Sebastiano Serlio
d) Gian Lorenzo Bernini

8. Which of these is one of the greatest examples of classical architecture known to man?

a) Reims Cathedral
b) The Parthenon
c) The Eiffel Tower
d) The Leaning Tower of Pisa

9. Which book is considered to be a seminal work of Postmodern architectural thought?

a) What Happens in Las Vegas
b) Journey to Cairo
c) Learning from Las Vegas
d) Like Water for Chocolate

10. Which architectural style did Frank Lloyd Wright first become famous for?

a) Prairie Style
b) Italianate architecture
c) Colonial Revival architecture
d) Rococo

031
TRANSPORT

1. Who designed the World Trade Center Transportation Hub that is situated in Lower Manhattan, NYC?

a) Emilio Tuñón
b) Carme Pigem
c) Santiago Calatrava
d) Ricardo Bofill

2. Karim Rashid designed a colourful metro station filled with cutting edge designs in which European city?

a) Naples
b) Paris
c) Madrid
d) Lisbon

3. Twenty three female statues adorn the facade of which popular train station in Paris?

a) Gare Rosa Parks
b) Gare du Nord
c) Javel
d) Avenue Henri Martin

4. Which acclaimed British architect is overseeing developments at the state-of-the-art Kuwait airport?

a) Jane Duncan
b) Nicholas Grimshaw
c) David Chipperfield
d) Norman Foster

5. Who designed the ornate subway station in Lisbon that boasts mirror-shine floor tiles, giant iron pillars, and a colourful ceiling made of Azulejos?

a) Raul Lino
b) Alvaro Siza
c) Tomás Taveira
d) Ricardo Bak Gordon

6. The Platform 9 3/4 scenes in the Harry Potter films were filmed at which London train station?

a) King's Cross station
b) Marylebone Station
c) London Bridge Station
d) Euston Station

7. In which year was the renowned Union Station in Washington D.C. completed?

a) 1923
b) 1907
c) 1899
d) 1912

8. Which airport won the 2018 Skytrax World's Best Airport award for the sixth consecutive year?

a) Paris Charles De Gaulle Airport
b) Oslo International Airport
c) Hong Kong International Airport
d) Singapore Changi Airport

9. Who designed Madrid's magnificent Estación de Atocha?

a) Rafael Moneo
b) Ricardo Bofill
c) Alberto de Palacio Elissagne
d) Santiago Calatrava

10. Which airport holds one of the largest collections of Pacific Northwest native American art in the world?

a) O'Hare International Airport
b) Vancouver International Airport
c) Fort Worth International Airport
d) JFK International Airport

032
POT LUCK

1. Maya Lin, who designed the Vietnam Veteran's Memorial in Washington D.C. is the niece of which famous Chinese architect?

a) Lu Wenyu
b) Lin Huiyin
c) Ma Yansong
d) Yu Wao

2. Which tower in Boston has had some of its windows randomly popping out ever since it was completed in 1972?

a) John Hancock Tower
b) Prudential Tower
c) Custom House Tower
d) One Financial Center

3. Which of these man-made structures are visible from space?

a) The Great Wall of China
b) The Pyramids of Giza
c) The Greenhouses of Almeria
d) All of them

4. Which U.S building generates more income from its observation decks than it's 85 floors of office space?

a) Trump Towers
b) One World Trade Center
c) Empire State Building
d) Willis Tower

5. Which U.S city has an abandoned subway system that was never used?

a) Chicago
b) Cincinnati
c) Atlanta
d) New York City

6. Which renowned architect was known to find 90-degree angles extremely uninteresting?

a) Zaha Hadid
b) Frank Lloyd Wright
c) Frank Gehry
d) David Ewart

7. The Marina Bay Sands in Singapore was built to resemble what?

a) A flight of stairs
b) A silo
c) A piano
d) A stack of playing cards

8. Who was affectionately known as 'God's architect'?

a) Louis Kahn
b) Rem Koolhaas
c) Antoni Gaudí
d) Renzo Piano

9. Who has been hailed "the greatest American architect of all time"?

a) Frank Lloyd Wright
b) Michael Graves
c) Robert Venturi
d) Frank Gehry

10. Who designed the Agora Garden in Taiwan?

a) Bob van Reeth
b) Vincent Callebaut
c) Paul Hankar
d) Lucien Kroll

033
WORLD'S TALLEST

1. **What is the tallest hotel in the world?**

a) Abraj Al Bait ZamZam Tower, Makkah
b) Burj Al Arab, Dubai
c) Baiyoke Tower II, Bangkok
d) Gevora Hotel, Dubai

2. **In which city would you find the tallest office building in the world?**

a) Dubai
b) Shanghai
c) New York City
d) Guangzhou

3. **What is the tallest university building in the world?**

a) Shinjuku Building, Kogakuin University
b) Main Building, Moscow State University
c) Wabash Building, Roosevelt University
d) Boissonade Tower, Hosei University

4. **How tall is the clock tower at Moscow State University?**

a) 288ft (88m)
b) 426ft (130m)
c) 387ft (118m)
d) 303ft (92m)

5. **At just over 500ft (152m) high, what is the tallest cross in the world?**

a) Great Cross of St. Augustine, Florida
b) Cross of All Nations, Lebanon
c) Third Millennium Cross of Coquimbo, Chile
d) Cross of the Valley of the Fallen, Spain

6. What is the world's tallest steel-supported brick building?

a) Empire State Building
b) Big Ben
c) Chrysler Building
d) Burj Khalifa

7. What is the highest dome in the world, standing 448ft (137m) from the ground?

a) St. Peter's Basilica, Vatican City
b) St Paul's Cathedral, London
c) The Blue Mosque, Istanbul
d) Dome of the Rock, Jerusalem

8. Where would you find the Ericsson Globe, the largest hemispherical building in the world?

a) Stockholm
b) Sydney
c) Oslo
d) Wellington

9. What is the tallest wooden structure in the world?

a) KDLT Tower
b) Gliwice Radio Tower
c) Warsaw Radio Mast
d) Emley Moor

10. Which building in India is the world's tallest brick minaret at 237.8ft (72.5m) tall?

a) Samatra TV Tower
b) Katanga TV Tower
c) Qutb Minar tower
d) Chand Minar

034
POT LUCK

1. What is Elvis Presley's colonial-style house in Memphis known as?

a) Graceland
b) House of Hope
c) Heartbreak Hotel
d) Rocklands

2. Andrew Carnegie donated a substantial amount of money towards the construction of what type of building?

a) Hospitals
b) Schools
c) Houses
d) Libraries

3. Which Disney castle is the oldest in the world?

a) Enchanted Stroybook Castle
b) Cinderella's Castle
c) Sleeping Beauty Castle
d) Beast's Castle

4. Where is the UNESCO World Heritage Site known as 'African Camelot'?

a) Ethiopia
b) Kenya
c) Zimbabwe
d) Malawi

5. The longest bridge in the world links which two prominent destinations?

a) Shenzhen and Zhongshan
b) Hong Kong and Macau
c) Kau Sai Chau and Hong Kong
d) Macau and Zhuhai

6. **Red tiled roofs and stuccoed walls are common features of which type of architecture?**

a) Tuscan
b) Classical
c) Mediterranean
d) Caribbean

7. **Who designed Banqueting House in Whitehall, London?**

a) Charles Barry
b) John Vanbrugh
c) Herbert Baker
d) Inigo Jones

8. **In which U.S, city would you find the fun, upside-down Wonderworks Museum?**

a) Orlando
b) Phoenix
c) Los Angeles
d) Houston

9. **What is the name of the space-age building located at Los Angeles International Airport (LAX)?**

a) Cosmos Building
b) Theme Building
c) Main Building
d) Galaxy Building

10. **Who designed the Mushroom House in Powder Mills Park, New York?**

a) Robert Venturi
b) Frank Gehry
c) James H. Johnson
d) David Ewart

035
ARCHITECTURAL HISTORY

1. Which period that was known as the 'age of awakening' also gave us Brunelleschi's Dome?

a) Renaissance
b) Classical
c) Gothic
d) Modern

2. What were the stepped pyramids designed by the Sumerian civilization in Mesopotamia and Persia known as?

a) Trusselets
b) Ziggurats
c) Agnerats
d) Pyradillions

3. Thin walls, flying buttresses, and large stained windows are all characteristics of which architectural style?

a) Neo-Modern
b) Romanesque
c) Gothic
d) Roman

4. Which of these was not a famous Renaissance architect?

a) Michelangelo Buonarroti
b) Donato Bramante
c) Leon Battista Alberti
d) Jules Hardouin

5. Which playful, decorative style of architecture followed the Baroque style of Louis XIV's court?

a) Rococo
b) Baroca
c) Neo-Baroque
d) Lococo

6. Neoclassical architecture was prevalent during which period?

a) 1600-1760
b) 1640-1850
c) 1720-1880
d) 1650-1790

7. When did work on the United States Capitol Building begin?

a) 1849
b) 1658
c) 1793
d) 1823

8. Which architectural style was especially popular between 1925 and 1940?

a) De-constructivism
b) Art Nouveau
c) Bauhaus design
d) Art Deco

9. Which of these is an example of ecclesiastical Gothic Architecture?

a) Cologne Cathedral
b) St Paul's Cathedral
c) The Guggenheim Museum
d) Westminster Abbey

10. When was Steel-frame Skyscraper Architecture particularly popular worldwide?

a) 1850-1950
b) 1900-2000
c) 1600-1700
d) 1780-1880

036
POT LUCK

1. What is the dome at the top of the Reichstag Building in Germany made from?

a) Wood
b) Copper
c) Glass
d) Brass

2. How old was Maya Lin when she designed the Vietnam Memorial?

a) 21
b) 27
c) 30
d) 34

3. What nickname was given to an old Standard Oil plant in 1924 after everyone who worked there was hospitalized for insanity?

a) The Madhouse
b) The Loony Gas Building
c) Crazy Quarters
d) Insanity Central

4. How long did it take to construct the Pentagon in Washington D.C?

a) 8 month
b) 20 months
c) 36 months
d) 16 months

5. Which Alaskan landmark was closed down by firemarshalls for not having smoke detectors?

a) Buckner Building
b) Oscar Anderson Houe
c) Aurora Ice Hotel
d) Baranov Museum

6. What is the largest unreinforced concrete dome in the world to date?

a) The Pantheon
b) Taj Mahal
c) Florence Cathedral
d) Hagia Sophia

7. In what year did the Leaning Tower of Pisa Stop moving for the first time in its 800-year history?

a) 1998
b) 2001
c) 2010
d) 1985

8. Which pagoda is considered to be the oldest wooden building on the planet?

a) Tiger Hill Pagoda, China
b) Horyuji Pagoda, Japan
c) Leifeng Pagoda, China
d) Songyue Pagoda, China

9. In which city would you find the world's thinnest house which is just 4 feet wide?

a) Paris
b) Helsinki
c) Moscow
d) Warsaw

10. In which year was the interior of the White House rebuilt using concrete and steel instead of wood?

a) 1968
b) 1915
c) 1950
d) 1933

037
STARCHITECTS

1. Which starchitect designed the Fisher Center for the Performing Arts at Bard College?

a) Frank Gehry
b) Zaha Hadid
c) Frank Lloyd Wright
d) I.M. Pei

2. Which Yale University graduate designed the David S. Ingalls Rink at Yale University?

a) Daniel Burnham
b) Eero Saarinen
c) Steven Holl
d) Cass Gilbert

3. What is Le Corbusier's only building in the USA?

a) Harvard Art Museums at Harvard University
b) IST Building at Florida Polytechnic University
c) Carpenter Center at Harvard University
d) Meister Hall at Bronx Community College

4. How old was Zaha Hadid when she died?

a) 58
b) 65
c) 69
d) 72

5. Who designed the Richards Medical Research Laboratories at the University of Pennsylvania ?

a) Richard Meier
b) Philip Johnson
c) Frank Gehry
d) Louis Kahn

6. Who has been hailed the world's first real starchitect?

a) Frank Lloyd Wright
b) Santiago Calatrava
c) Christopher Wren
d) Alvaro Siza

7. Which of these is not one of Zaha Hadid's designs?

a) Louis Vuitton Foundation
b) Al Wahda Sports Center
c) Cardiff Bay Opera House
d) Salerno Maritime Terminal

8. What nationality is Minoru Yamasaki who designed the original World Trade Center in NYC?

a) Chinese
b) Japanese
c) American
d) Vietnamese

9. In which decade did journalists coin the term 'starchitect'?

a) 1960s
b) 1970s
c) 1980s
d) 1990s

10. Which starchitect designed the S. R. Crown Hall in Chicago, Illinois?

a) Carl Ludvig Engel
b) Leo von Klenze
c) Bruno Taut
d) Mies van der Rohe

038
POT LUCK

1. What is the once-beautiful Michigan Theatre is now used as?

a) Retail space & garage
b) Music school
c) Community college & dorms
d) Orphanage

2. Which popular NYC landmark is known to 'howl', 'moan' and 'whine' on a particularly windy day?

a) Empire State Building
b) Chrysler Builder
c) One World Trade Center
d) 432 Park Avenue

3. In which country was the Leaning Tower of Zaragoza located that was demolished in 1892?

a) France
b) Spain
c) Italy
d) Portugal

4. Which university building is modelled after Bhutanese monasteries, also known as Dzong architecture?

a) Duke University
b) University of Chicago
c) Stanford University
d) University of Texas

5. In which U.S state would you find the 234ft (71m) tall Phoenix Shot Tower?

a) Maryland
b) New Jersey
c) Arizona
d) Georgia

6. **What is the world's tallest monumental column, standing 567.31ft (173m) high?**

a) Astoria Column
b) Washington Monument
c) San Jacinto Monument
d) Civil War Memorial

7. **What 'absolutely fireproof' building was destroyed in what is still the deadliest single-building fire in U.S. history?**

a) Grace Cathedral
b) Iroquois Theater
c) Sears Tower
d) Beverly Hills Supper Club

8. **What is the tallest free-standing tower in the world?**

a) Long Ta, China
b) Almaty Tower, Kazakhstan
c) West Pearl Tower, China
d) Tokyo Sky Tree, Japan

9. **Which architect wrote the book 'Complexity and Contradiction in Architecture'?**

a) Robert Venturi
b) Will Pryce
c) Frank Ching
d) Ross King

10. **At a height of 550ft (168m), what is the tallest Ferris Wheel in the world?**

a) Singapore Flyer, Singapore
b) Star of Nanchang, China
c) High Roller, Las Vegas
d) Ferris Wheel of Fortune, Chicago

039
SHAPES

1. Which blocks were developed to help children learn about geometric forms, maths, and creative designs?

a) Macintosh Blocks
b) Fritzer Blocks
c) Steinhaus Blocks
d) Froebel Blocks

2. Which shape is a closed plane figure, formed by 3 or more line segments that intersect only at their endpoints?

a) Pentagon
b) Polygon
c) Hexagon
d) Circle

3. Equilateral is one of the most common forms of which shape frequently used in architecture?

a) Triangle
b) Rectangle
c) Square
d) Circle

4. Diamonds, triangles, and arches were very popular in which architectural style?

a) Art Deco
b) Gothic
c) Tudor
d) Modern

5. What are the flowing lines associated with Art Nouveau sometimes refered to as?

a) Waves
b) Soundsilence
c) Headthump
d) Whiplash

6. **What shapes were used in the East Building in the National Gallery of Art in Washington D.C?**

a) Right triangles
b) Isosceles triangles
c) Scalene triangles
d) Heptagons

7. **In what shape is the United States Department of Defense as well as the Castle of Good Hope in Cape Town built?**

a) Rectangle
b) Square
c) Hexagon
d) Pentagon

8. **What shape is the Blue Room, the President's office at the White House?**

a) Oval
b) Round
c) Square
d) Triangular

9. **What are the set of innovative houses designed by Piet Blom and built in Rotterdam known as?**

a) Squared
b) The Squares
c) Cube Houses
d) The Rotter-Cubes

10. **Who designed the United States Air Force Academy's Cadet Chapel in Colourado Springs that sports an impressive tetrahedron frame?**

a) Michael Graves
b) Walter Netsch
c) Peter Eisenman
d) Eero Saarinen

040
POT LUCK

1. Who designed the Kresge Auditorium at the Massachusetts Institute of Technology?

a) Eero Saarinen
b) Lars Sonck
c) Viljo Revell
d) Timo Penttila

2. Which Chinese landmark is also known as 'Wanli Changcheng'?

a) Terracotta Warriors Museum
b) Summer Palace
c) The Great Wall of China
d) Forbidden City

3. Where in the UK is the Eden Project, the world's largest greenhouse project?

a) Derbyshire
b) Morayshire
c) Gwent
d) Cornwall

4. Which American architect-engineer invented the geodesic dome construction?

a) Thom Mayne
b) Buckminster Fuller
c) David Childs
d) William van Alen

5. Where can the Suvarnabhumi Airport control tower, the world's tallest, be found?

a) Bangkok
b) Hanoi
c) Manila
d) Kuala Lumpur

6. Which English cathedral has the highest spire?

a) York Minster
b) Wells Cathedral
c) Salisbury Cathedral
d) Ely Cathedral

7. How tall is the Spire of Dublin that opened in January, 2003?

a) 320.1ft (97.6m)
b) 226.7ft (69.1m)
c) 452.9ft (138.0m)
d) 397.6ft (121.2m)

8. What is the name of the fictional character that lived in the Notre-Dame Cathedral?

a) Horatio
b) Quasimodo
c) Siegfried
d) Belthazar

9. Who designed the Great Florence Cathedral Dome?

a) Filippo Brunelleschi
b) Gio Ponti
c) Massimiliano Fuksas
d) Carlo Maderno

10. Gilbert Cass designed which popular building in NYC?

a) 601 Lexington Avenue
b) 35 Hudson Yards
c) Woolworth Building
d) One57

041
POT LUCK

1. Who designed the Fisher Center for Performing Arts in New York?

a) Frank Gehry
b) Eero Saarinen
c) Ross King
d) David Chipperfield

2. Which bridge features the world's longest bridge fountain known as the Moonlight Rainbow Fountain?

a) Busan Harbor Bridge
b) Banpo Bridge
c) Gwangan Bridge
d) Banghwa Bridge

3. What is the name of the world's largest treehouse that can be found in Crossville, Tennessee?

a) The Senator's Treehouse
b) The King's Treehouse
c) The President's Treehouse
d) The Minister's Treehouse

4. Which term refers to a curved shape that results in a lower pitch at the bottom of a roof slope?

a) Bonneted
b) Bay
c) Bellcast
d) Buttress

5. Which of these buildings were not designed by Jørn Utzon?

a) Sydney Opera House
b) J. Paul Getty Museum
c) Paustian Showroom
d) Kuwait National Assembly

6. Which of these architects is not associated with Googie and Tiki architecture?

a) Inigo Jones
b) Paul Williams
c) Eldon Davis
d) Wayne McAllister

7. Who designed the Robot Building that houses the United Overseas Bank's Bangkok headquarters?

a) Kris Yao
b) Sumet Jumsai
c) Roan Ching-yueh
d) Arthur Huang

8. Which housing style was very popular in the USA between 1600 and 1740?

a) Dutch Colonial
b) Tuscan
c) New England Colonial
d) Cape Cod Style

9. In which English county would you find Windsor Castle?

a) Warwickshire
b) Sussex
c) Yorkshire
d) Berkshire

10. When did excavation begin for the original world Trade Center twin towers?

a) 1966
b) 1974
c) 1958
d) 1963

042
POT LUCK

1. Who, after Walter Gropius and Hannes Meyer, was the third director of the Bauhaus School of Design?

a) Albert Speer
b) Paul Wallot
c) Leo von Klenze
d) Mies van der Rohe

2. The term 'International Style' was coined by which American architect?

a) Daniel Burnham
b) Philip Johnson
c) Steven Holl
d) Cass Gilbert

3. Frank Lloyd Wright designed the lobby of which Chicago landmark?

a) The Rookery Building
b) Monadnock Building
c) Aon Center
d) Prudential Plaza

4. What is the popular Kaufmann Residence in Pennsylvania, designed by Frank Lloyd Wright, also known as?

a) Fallingwater
b) Waterfalls
c) Bubblingbrook
d) Rushingwaters

5. Why was British architect John Poulson sentenced to five years in prison in the 1970s?

a) Murder
b) Theft
c) Bribery
d) Assault

6. What is the name given to small tooth like projections that adorn the area under an overhang?

a) Cupola
b) Dentils
c) Dormer
d) Finial

7. In what year was the Pritzker Prizer founded?

a) 1979
b) 1968
c) 1972
d) 1981

8. At what institution did Art Garfunkel major in architecture?

a) Vanderbilt University
b) Penn State University
c) University of Notre Dame
d) Columbia University

9. What name was given to the futuristic, "Space Age" building style that was popular in the U.S during the 1950s and 1960s?

a) Googie
b) Doogie
c) Boogie
d) Woogie

10. Which of these did Philip Johnson not design?

a) JFK Memorial, Texas
b) Seagram Building, New York
c) Tribune Tower, Chicago
d) Transco Tower, Texas

043
POT LUCK

1. Which building in Chicago was designed and built for the 1893 World's Columbian Exposition?

a) Chicago Board of Trade Building
b) Chicago's Museum of Science and Industry
c) Reliance Building
d) Marquette Building

2. James Gandon and Thomas Cooley designed which famous building in Dublin, Ireland?

a) Four Courts
b) Dublin Castle
c) Liberty Hall
d) Muckross House

3. Where was American Gothic architecture imported from?

a) Spain
b) France
c) United Kingdom
d) Italy

4. Which of these is not a prestigious prize in the field of architecture?

a) RIBA Award
b) Aga Khan Award
c) Pritzker Prize
d) Abel Prize

5. Which architect redesigned the city of London after the devastating fires of 1666?

a) Charles Barry
b) Christopher Wren
c) Nicholas Hawksmoor
d) James Wyatt

6. Who said: "Create beautiful things. That's all"

a) Philip Johnson
b) Frank Gehry
c) Paul Goldberger
d) Ariel Aufgang

7. Who designed the Texas Capitol?

a) Thomas Ustick Walter
b) Frederick Law Olmsted
c) Elijah E. Myers
d) Bertram Goodhue

8. In which U.S. city would you find the multi-purpose stadium known as the Astrodome?

a) Austin
b) Dallas
c) San Antonio
d) Houston

9. What do you call the triangular end of a wall above the eaves with a peaked roof?

a) Gable
b) Fable
c) Sable
d) Lable

10. What is the world's tallest free-standing masonry structure?

a) Python Smelter Stack
b) Anaconda Smelter Stack
c) Viper Smelter Stack
d) Adder Smelter Stack

044
POT LUCK

1. At which London landmark would you find the Whispering Gallery?

a) Tower of London
b) St Paul's Cathedral
c) Buckingham Palace
d) The Gherkin

2. Which historical landmark in Galveston, Texas was designed by Nicholas J. Clayton?

a) Bishop's Palace
b) Wyly Theatre
c) Ruby City
d) Baker Hotel

3. How tall is the CN Tower in Toronto, Canada?

a) 1,815ft (553m)
b) 1,750ft (533m)
c) 1,265ft (386m)
d) 1,983ft (604m)

4. In which African city would you find the Hassan II Mosque?

a) Casablanca
b) Kampala
c) Maseru
d) Nairobi

5. Which museum in Maryland is a landmark example of German Colonial Architecture?

a) Visionary Art Museum
b) Schifferstadt Architectural Museum
c) Annmarie Sculpture Garden & Arts Center
d) Harriet Tubman Mueum

6. Which architectural style was the Art Institute of Chicago designed in?

a) Tudor
b) Greek Revival
c) Art Deco
d) Beaux-Arts style

7. In which year was the Prague astronomical clock first installed?

a) 1385
b) 1625
c) 1410
d) 1510

8. In which city in the USA would you find the Hollywood Bowl amphitheater?

a) Nashville
b) Chicago
c) New York City
d) Los Angeles

9. What is the largest castle in the UK?

a) Edinburgh Castle
b) Arundel Castle
c) Windsor Castle
d) Corfe Castle

10. Which American architect was almost evangelical about Gothic Revival architecture?

a) Alexander Jackson Davis
b) Raymond Hood
c) Thomas Phifer
d) James Garrison

045
POT LUCK

1. Which popular German attraction features 43 bells and 32 life-sized figures that come to life at 11am every day?

a) Black Forest Glockenspiel
b) Rathaus-Glockenspiel
c) Berlin Glockenspiel
d) Munich Glockenspiel

2. What is the nickname of the Joseph Chamberlain Memorial Clock Tower that stands at the University of Birmingham, UK?

a) Tick-Tock Joe
b) Tall Joe
c) Big Joe
d) Old Joe

3. Who designed the Rajabai Clock Tower in Mumbai, India?

a) George Gilbert Scott
b) Charles Barry
c) Michael Hopkins
d) Joseph Paxton

4. Who designed the Trinity Church in downtown Boston which is considered to be a iteration of the Episcopal church?

a) Ralph Adams Cram
b) Stanford White
c) Henry Hobson Richardson
d) Bertram Goodhue

5. Which of these Japanese buildings were not designed by Tadao Ando?

a) Tokyo Skytree
b) Yoyogi National Gymnasium
c) Omotesando Hills
d) 21_21 Design Sight Museum

6. In which country will you find the Anne Frank House, the building dedicated to Jewish wartime diarist Anne Frank?

a) Netherlands
b) Belgium
c) Poland
d) Russia

7. Who designed the New National Stadium in Tokyo for the postponed 2020 Olympic Games?

a) Shin Takamatsu
b) Shigeru Ban
c) Toyo Ito
d) Kengo Kuma

8. What are the seven tall buildings in Russia of Stalinist design more commonly known as?

a) Seven Brothers
b) Seven Giants
c) Seven Sisters
d) Seven Friends

9. Who designed Carnegie Hall in New York?

a) William Burnet Tuthill
b) Louis Kahn
c) Frank Gehry
d) Denise Scott Brown

10. What name is given to the mixture of Spanish, Christian, and Muslim architecture?

a) Romanesque
b) Moorish Revival
c) Mudejar
d) Mannerism

046
POT LUCK

1. Who designed the church of San Giorgio Maggiore in Venice?

a) Filippo Brunelleschi
b) Andrea Palladio
c) Leon Alberti
d) Vincenzo Scamozzi

2. The Lung Center in the Philippines was designed by which esteemed architect?

a) Froilan Hong
b) Lance Fuscili
c) George Ramos
d) Gabriel Formoso

3. Which of these is not a renowned Spanish architect?

a) Raul Lino
b) Carme Pinos
c) Rafael Moneo
d) Santiago Calatrava

4. What is a circular moulding also known as?

a) Spherix
b) Roundel
c) Ringdun
d) Circlet

5. In which Italian city would you find the Mole Antonelliana, the tallest museum in the world?

a) Naples
b) Florence
c) Turin
d) Verona

6. Who designed the Bonifacio Monument in the Philippines?

a) Guillermo Tolentino
b) Tomas Mapua
c) Felino Palafox
d) Pablo Antonio

7. Which of these is not an example of Byzantine architecture?

a) Hagia Irene
b) Basilica of San Vitale
c) Hagia Sophia
d) Church of the All Saints

8. Which Spanish architect's work includes Casa Mila, Casa Baltto and Casa Vicenc?

a) Antonio Gaudi
b) Mario Botta
c) Carlo Scarpa
d) Alvar Aato

9. Who was the architect of the Erechtheion in Athens?

a) Ictinus
b) Mnesicles
c) Callicrates
d) Cossutius

10. What is the term given to a sculptural embellishment of an arch?

a) Aisle
b) Façade
c) Accolade
d) Abacus

047
POT LUCK

1. Where in Greece would you find the Church of Saint Catherine?

a) Parga
b) Thessaloniki
c) Assos
d) Plaka

2. Where are the headquarters of the American Institute of Architects (AIA)?

a) Washington D.C.
b) New York City
c) Chicago
d) Jamestown

3. Which Mexican architect designed the futuristic Museo Soumaya museum in Mexico?

a) Mauricio Rocha
b) Fernando Romero
c) Enrique Norten
d) Alberto Kalach

4. Jean Chalgrin designed which prominent French landmark?

a) Palais Garnier
b) Eiffel Tower
c) Palace of Versailles
d) Arc de Triomphe

5. How many floors does the Shanghai World Financial Center have?

a) 101
b) 91
c) 111
d) 121

6. What is the tallest building ever to be demolished in London?

a) Southwark Towers
b) The Elephant's Castle
c) Vlad's Skyscraper
d) Chelsea View

7. In Which U.S state would you find the Albert Einstein planetarium, located inside the National Air and Space Museum?

a) San Francisco
b) Chicago
c) Washington D.C
d) Los Angeles

8. In which Scandinavian city would you find the Turning Torso, the world's first twisting skyscraper?

a) Aarhus
b) Aalborg
c) Bergen
d) Malmö

9. What do you call the sharp edge where two surfaces meet at an angle?

a) Farris
b) Arris
c) Cornice
d) Belt

10. Which architectural term refers to a free-standing bell tower?

a) Campanile
b) Cellula
c) Triforium
d) Balaza

048
POT LUCK

1. Which architectural feature was named after French architect Francois Mansart?

a) Mansard Roof
b) Mansard Trusses
c) Mansard Bridge
d) Mansard Stairs

2. What is the most widely-used building material in the world?

a) Cement
b) Bricks
c) Concrete
d) Wood

3. A tall spire known as a mineret is common in which type of architecture?

a) Spanish architcture
b) Islamic architecture
c) Italian architecture
d) Greek architecture

4. Which nickname was given to the Casa de los Azulejos of Mexico City?

a) House of Pictures
b) The Blue House
c) House of Tiles
d) The Block House

5. Alfred Messel designed the first German store to be built entirely of what?

a) Stone, steel, glass
b) Concrete, glass, brass
c) Brick, cement, steel
d) Steel, glass, wood

6. What is the oldest surviving collection of settlements in West Africa?

a) Waka Tifaldo
b) Gritchit Vale
c) Dhar Tichitt
d) Hubra Calandre

7. What is the name given to projecting fins or canopies that shade windows from direct sunlight?

a) Cellas
b) Bressummers
c) Bulwarks
d) Brise soleil

8. In which Italian city would you find the Rialto Bridge?

a) Venice
b) Rome
c) Milan
d) Florence

9. Which of the following architectural styles uses materials such as stainless steel and aluminium?

a) Imperialism
b) Art Deco
c) Baroque
d) Gothic

10. At which Japanese institute does Kengo Kuma teach and run an architectural research lab?

a) Osaka University
b) Kansai University
c) Tokyo University
d) Waseda University

049
ARCHITECTURAL EDUCATION

1. At which U.S university did Frank Gehry study?

a) Harvard University
b) Midwestern University
c) Princeton University
d) Stanford University

2. Who designed the Library and Learning Center at Vienna University of Economics?

a) Frank Lloyd Wright
b) Zaha Hadid
c) Renzo Piano
d) Norman Foster

3. At which U.S university would you find the McGraw Tower?

a) UCLA
b) Duke University
c) Cornell University
d) Northwestern University

4. Who designed Eton College - the school attended by both Prince William and Prince Harry?

a) James Wyatt
b) Augustus Pugin
c) Norman Foster
d) John Shaw Jr

5. What is the Sather Tower that is located on the Berkeley campus of the University of California, also known as?

a) Campanile
b) Totenhole
c) McAllister's Spear
d) The Grotto

6. At which university did Louis Kahn teach from 1957 until the time of his death?

a) Columbia University
b) University of Pennsylvania
c) Vanderbilt University
d) Boston University

7. Where did Renzo Piano study architecture?

a) Bocconi University
b) University of Turin
c) Milan Polytechnic University
d) University of Palermo

8. Which U.S. university is home to Beinecke Library that houses around 500,000 books and several million manuscripts?

a) Yale University
b) Penn State University
c) Texas A&M University
d) Clemson University

9. Where did David Chipperfield graduate from in 1977?

a) Manchester School of Architecture
b) Portsmouth School of Architecture
c) Kingston School of Art
d) Architectural Association School in London

10. Which of these architects did not contribute to the design of Nassau Hall at Princeton University?

a) John Notman
b) Louis Kahn
c) Benjamin Henry Latrobe
d) Robert Smith

050
POT LUCK

1. What is the name given to the main body of a church where the congregation are usually seated?

a) Transept
b) Nave
c) Aisle
d) Apse

2. Where in London, is the Princess of Wales Memorial Fountain located?

a) Greenwich Park
b) Regent's Park
c) Hyde Park
d) St James's Park

3. Who designed the Kullen Lighthouse in Sweden?

a) Axel Haig
b) Magnus Dahlander
c) Carl Westman
d) Axel Anderberg

4. Who does the Statue of Unity in India depict?

a) Sardar Vallabhbhai Patel
b) Rahul Gandhi
c) Rajnath Singh
d) Arvind Kejriwal

5. Who said: "Recognizing the need is the primary condition for design."?

a) Rem Koolhaas
b) Charles Eames
c) Walter Gropius
d) Mies van der Rohe

Answers to 049

1. a) Harvard University
2. b) Zaha Hadid
3. c) Cornell University
4. d) John Shaw Jr

5. a) Campanile
6. b) University of Pennsylvania
7. c) Milan Polytechnic University

8. a) Yale University
9. d) Architectural Association School in London
10. b) Louis Kahn

6. What year saw the opening of the Quadracci Pavilion at the Milwaukee Art Museum?

a) 2012
b) 1998
c) 2009
d) 2001

7. How tall is the Duke University Bell tower?

a) 210ft (64m)
b) 300ft (91m)
c) 178ft (54m)
d) 165ft (50m)

8. What is Westminster Abbey in London predominantly constructed from?

a) Concrete
b) Portland stone
c) Bath Stone
d) Sandstone

9. Which architect combined Modernism and Populism in works she built mainly in Brazil?

a) Zaha Hadid
b) Julia Morgan
c) Lina Bo Bardi
d) Clarice Lispector

10. Which of the following architectural styles is not American in origin?

a) Arts and Crafts Movement
b) Rustic
c) American Craftsman
d) Cape Cod

PICTURE ROUND #1
ARCHITECT SKETCHES

Can you name the eight architects depicted in the following sketches?

1

2

3

4

Answers to 050

1. b) Nave
2. c) Hyde Park
3. b) Magnus Dahlander
4. a) Sardar Vallabhbhai Patel

5. b) Charles Eames
6. d) 2001
7. a) 210ft (64m)
8. b) Portland stone

9. c) Lina Bo Bardi
10. a) Arts and Crafts
    Movement

5

6

7

8

PICTURE ROUND #2
BUILDING SKETCHES

Can you name the eight buildings depicted in the following sketches?

1

2

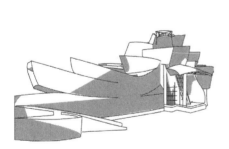

3

4

Answers to Picture Round #1

1. Rem Koolhaas
2. Richard Rogers
3. Norman Foster
4. Nicholas Grimshaw

5. Zaha Hadid
6. Peter Zumthor
7. Alvar Aalto
8. Bjarke Ingles

5

6

7

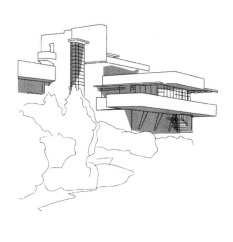

8

PICTURE ROUND #3
ARCHITECT SKETCHES

Can you name the eight architects depicted in the following sketches?

1

2

3

4

Answers to Picture Round #2

1. The Eden Project
2. The Solomon R. Guggenheim Museum
3. Guggenheim Museum Bilbao
4. Burj Khalifa

5. Bauhaus Dessau
6. The Einstein Tower (Einsteinturm)
7. Empire State Building
8. Fallingwater

5

6

7

8

PICTURE ROUND #4
BUILDING SKETCHES

Can you name the eight buildings depicted in the following sketches?

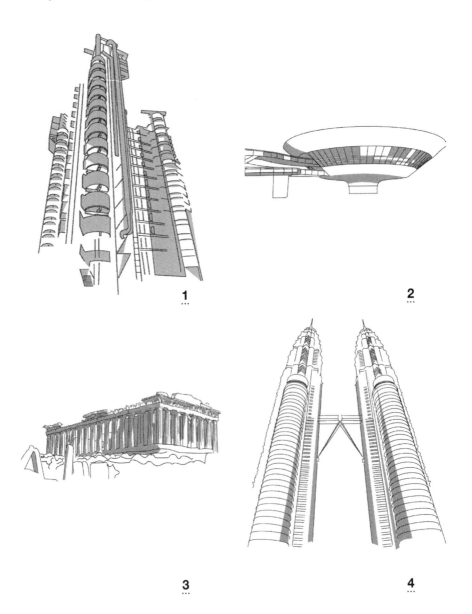

1
...

2
...

3
...

4
...

Answers to Picture Round #3

1. Amanda Levette
2. Mies van der Rohe
3. David Chipperfield
4. David Adjaye

5. Louis Kahn
6. Daniel Libeskind
7. Frank Ghery
8. Le Corbusier
 (Charles-Édouard Jeanneret)

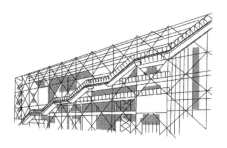

5

6

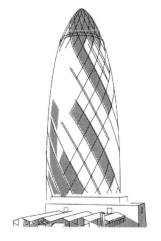

7

8

051
POT LUCK

1. Who designed the Jewish Museum in NYC?

a) Frank Gehry
b) C.P.H. Gilbert
c) Norman Foster
d) Philip Johnson

2. Who said: "Not many architects have the luxury to reject significant things." ?

a) Bjarke Ingels
b) Tadao Ando
c) Charles Eames
d) Rem Koolhaas

3. What do you call the three-dimensional spandrels that support the weight of a dome?

a) Pendentive
b) Phiale
c) Peristyle
d) Parapet

4. What is London's Leadenhall Building also known as?

a) The Slope
b) The Cheesegrater
c) The Bucket
d) The Turntable

5. What famous statue can be found at Piccadilly Circus in London?

a) Statue of Poseidon
b) Statue of Hades
c) Statue of Zeus
d) Statue of Eros

6. Which architectural style does the Goelet Building in NYC represent?

a) Classical
b) Prairie School
c) Art Deco
d) Victorian

7. In what year was the Sydney Harbour Bridge built?

a) 1934
b) 1923
c) 1917
d) 1942

8. How long did it take to complete the Empire State Building?

a) One year 45 days
b) One year 139 days
c) Two years 19 days
d) Three years 87 days

9. Which statue depicting Gautama Buddha is the third-tallest in the world?

a) Tian Tan Buddha
b) Laykyun Setkyar
c) Leshan Giant
d) Gal Vihara

10. The Thompson Memorial Library can be found at which elite college in the U.S?

a) Amherst College
b) Colby College
c) Williams College
d) Vassar College

052
POT LUCK

1. Which of these architects did not design the Sydney Harbour Bridge?

a) John Bradfield
b) Philip Cox
c) Ralph Freeman
d) Thomas S. Tait

2. How long did it take to complete the Emperors Yan and Huang Statue in China?

a) 20 years
b) 5 years
c) 10 years
d) 15 years

3. At which college in the U.S will you find the Cutler Majestic Theatre?

a) Swarthmore College
b) Colby College
c) Reed College
d) Emerson College

4. In what year did the Whitney Museum of American Art open in the Marcel Breuer designed building on Madison Avenue?

a) 1948
b) 1957
c) 1963
d) 1937

5. Where can the controversial Boutique Monaco be found?

a) Seoul
b) Busan
c) Ulsan
d) Daegu

6. Which material is the Pantheon's dome constructed from?

a) Stone
b) Concrete
c) Glass
d) Wood

7. Who designed the Scott Monument, dedicated to Scottish author Sir Walter Scott?

a) George Meikle Kemp
b) George Wittet
c) James Gibbs
d) William Adam

8. What is a masonry of big blocks cut with even faces and square edges known as?

a) Basement
b) Barage
c) Arris
d) Ashlar

9. What do you call a large, high circular hall or room in a building?

a) Rib vault
b) Roof comb
c) Rotunda
d) Rake

10. Who said: "Architecture is a visual art and the buildings speak for themselves"?

a) Denise Scott Brown
b) Julia Morgan
c) Jeanne Gang
d) Carol Ross Barney

053
POT LUCK

1. In which year was the National Firefighters Memorial in London opened?

a) 1991
b) 1997
c) 2001
d) 2005

2. Which term describes the flow of people throughout a building?

a) Swim
b) Stream
c) Circulation
d) Wind

3. When was the cornerstone of the White House laid?

a) October 1792
b) January 1855
c) March 1725
d) July 1864

4. Which Russian statue is dedicated to the Battle of Stalingrad?

a) Russia Our Home
b) The Motherland Calls
c) For the Motherland
d) Hope Prevails

5. Which word describes the lowest voussoir on each side of an arch?

a) Spandrel
b) Spere
c) Spire
d) Springer

6. In which city would you find the American Museum of Natural History?

a) New York City
b) Chicago
c) Los Angeles
d) Jacksonville

7. Who designed the Mansueto Library at the University of Chicago?

a) Albert Speer
b) Helmut Jahn
c) Hans Scharoun
d) Adolf Meyer

8. Which church has the longest nave in England?

a) Wells Cathedral
b) St Paul's Cathedral
c) St Albans Cathedral
d) Ely Cathedral

9. When was the Golden Gate Bridge built?

a) 1933
b) 1944
c) 1922
d) 1955

10. Which architect said: "Architecture starts when you carefully put two bricks together. There it begins"

a) Stanford White
b) William Pereira
c) Mies van der Rohe
d) James Polshek

054
POT LUCK

1. When was the Brooklyn Museum in New York City built?

a) 1895
b) 1905
c) 1880
d) 1909

2. Which word is used to describe the stonework elements that support the glass in a Gothic window?

a) Tracery
b) Lacery
c) Suburst
d) Stoop

3. Which famous building in NYC did Andy Warhol feature in an eight hour long documentary?

a) Trump Towers
b) Empire State Building
c) One World Trade Center
d) Chrysler Building

4. How tall is New York's Freedom Tower?

a) 1885ft (575m)
b) 1548ft (472m)
c) 1776ft (541m)
d) 1224ft (373m)

5. How long is the Golden Gate Bridge in San Francisco?

a) 2.1 miles (3.37km)
b) 1.7 miles (2.74km)
c) 1.2 miles (1.93km)
d) 1.5 miles (2.41km)

6. How many degrees does the Leaning Tower of Pisa lean?

a) Four
b) Seven
c) Five
d) Nine

7. Who designed the Dugald Stewart Monument in Edinburgh?

a) John Vanbrugh
b) William Henry Playfair
c) James Wyatt
d) William Kent

8. Who was quoted as saying: "Good buildings come from good people and all problems are solved by good design."?

a) Augustus Pugin
b) William Kent
c) John Soane
d) Stephen Gardiner

9. When were renovations to the University of Michigan's (U-M's) Michigan Stadium completed?

a) 2011
b) 2009
c) 2017
d) 2005

10. In what year was the African Renaissance Monument in Senegal completed?

a) 2012
b) 2010
c) 1998
d) 2002

055
POT LUCK

1. When was Frank Lloyd Wright born?

   a) 8 June 1867
   b) 7 April 1856
   c) 23 August 1884
   d) 12 January 1862

2. Who designed the Welsh National War Memorial that was unveiled by the Prince of Wales in 1928?

   a) William Young
   b) David MacGibbon
   c) Ninian Comper
   d) Archibald Leitch

3. In which year was the Metropolitan Museum of Art, in NYC founded?

   a) 1854
   b) 1870
   c) 1901
   d) 1910

4. What is the name given to the city normally built around North African citadels?

   a) Outer City
   b) Inner City
   c) Casbah
   d) Favela

5. How long did it take to construct the Eiffel Tower?

   a) 5 years
   b) 2 years
   c) 7 years
   d) 1 year

6. The Christ the Redeemer statue in Rio de Janerio is clad in mosaic of thousands of triangular tiles made from what?

a) Soapstone
b) Clay
c) Ceramic
d) Glass

7. Who designed Hearst Castle, California, which opened in 1919?

a) Walter Griffin
b) Robert Venturi
c) Julia Morgan
d) Cass Gilbert

8. Characters from which popular TV series lived at Durfee Hall at Yale University?

a) Greek
b) Gilmore Girls
c) Glee
d) Gossip Girl

9. What do you call a spiral, scroll-like ornament that forms the base of the Ionic order?

a) Volute
b) Tympanum
c) Transom
d) Undercroft

10. Which Mexican architect said: "Any work of architecture which does not express serenity is a mistake"?

a) Michel Rojkind
b) Fernando Romero
c) Alberto Kalach
d) Luis Barragan

056
POT LUCK

1. Aston Webb and Thomas Brock designed which London monument to honour Queen Victoria?

a) Victoria Memorial
b) Queen Victoria Legacy Memorial
c) Ode to a Queen
d) The Royal Memorial

2. What was the first skyscraper in the world to feature wind turbines?

a) Empire State Building
b) Burj Khalifa
c) Tokyo Skytree
d) Bahrein World Trade Center

3. What is another name for the cornerstones of brick or stone walls?

a) Quance
b) Quoin
c) Pteroma
d) Portico

4. In which year did Frank Lloyd Wright's Guggenheim Museum open?

a) 1959
b) 1949
c) 1939
d) 1969

5. Which architectural style is known to combine elements from other popular styles?

a) Revivalism
b) Neonism
c) Subtlism
d) Eclecticism

6. How many stained glass windows does the Duke University Chapel have?

a) 85
b) 62
c) 77
d) 98

7. Which famous architect was born on 28 February 1929?

a) Frank Gehry
b) Louis Kahn
c) David Chipperfield
d) Zaha Hadid

8. Who was quoted as saying: "Architecture is not about space but about time"?

a) Robert Venturi
b) Vito Acconel
c) Peter Eisenman
d) Albert Kahn

9. How long did it take to complete the Christ the Redeemer statue in Brazil?

a) 17 years
b) 12 years
c) 9 years
d) 7 years

10. What material is the Statue of Liberty made from?

a) Copper
b) Bronze
c) Steel
d) Wood

057
CATHEDRALS #2

1. Which of these cathedrals has a masonry dome?

a) St Peter's Basilica, Vatican City
b) Saint Basil's Cathedral, Moscow
c) St Paul Cathedral, London
d) Santa Maria del Fiore, Florence

2. Which is considered to be the largest cathedral in the world?

a) Cologne Cathedral
b) Seville Cathedral
c) Notre Dame de Paris
d) Milan Cathedral

3. Who designed the cathedral of Seville?

a) Alfonso Alvares
b) Juan de Castillo
c) Filippo Terzi
d) Filippo Bruneleschi

4. What is the architectural style of Westminster Abbey?

a) Gothic architecture
b) Renaissance architecture
c) Baroque architecture
d) Tented-roof church

5. How many towers does the Cathedral de Notre Dame have?

a) 3
b) 4
c) 1
d) 2

6. When did the construction of Sagrada Familia in Barcelona officially begin?

a) 1882
b) 1883
c) 1884
d) 1885

7. Which British royals married at St. Paul's Cathedral in London?

a) Prince Elizabeth and Prince Philip
b) Prince William and Kate Middleton
c) Prince Charles and Lady Diana
d) Prince Harry and Meghan Markle

8. How many cathedrals are there in the Vatican City?

a) 10
b) 15
c) 20
d) 25

9. Which of these Cathedrals was built first?

a) San Lorenzo Cathedral, Milan
b) Santa Maria in Trastevere, Rome
c) St. Peter's Basilica, Rome
d) Etchmiadzin Cathedral, Armenia

10. Which of these features are not found in a cathedral?

a) Narthex
b) Aisle
c) Minaret
d) Nave

058
MODERN ARCHITECTS

1. Which of these architects have used reinforced concrete and modular systems of standard sized units?

a) Le Corbusier
b) Antoni Gaudi
c) Renzo Piano
d) Jean Nouvel

2. Where did Zaha Hadid study architecture?

a) ETH Zurich
b) University College London
c) Architectural Association
d) RMIT University

3. Who is considered to be "the father of modernism" in architecture?

a) Frank Gehry
b) Philip Johnson
c) Louis Sullivan
d) Tom Wright

4. Who designed the Pyramide du Louvre?

a) I. M. Pei
b) Ludwig Mies Van Der Rohe
c) Moshe Safdie
d) Zaha Hadid

5. Which of these buildings is not design by Tom Wright?

a) Burj Al Arab, Dubai
b) Capital Gate, Abu Dhabi
c) Ribbon of Light, Iran
d) Dancing House, Czech Republic

6. Which of these modern architects is the founder of the Bauhaus School?

a) Alvar Alto
b) Walter Gropius
c) Marcel Lajos Breuer
d) Robert Mallet-Stevens

7. Which Japanese architect was awarded the Pritzker prize in 2019?

a) Arata Isozaki
b) Toyo Ito
c) Kengo Kuma
d) Tadao Ando

8. Which architectural designer's work is known for its minimalist aesthetic?

a) Daniel Libeskind
b) Peter Eisenman
c) John Pawson
d) Rem Koolhaas

9. Who designed the Barcelona Pavilion?

a) Luis Barragan
b) Ludwig Mies van der Rohe
c) Oscar Niemeyer
d) Alvar Aalto

10. Which architect designed Fallingwater House, one of the most iconic buildings of modern architecture?

a) Tom Wright
b) Renzo Piano
c) Zaha Hadid
d) Frank Lloyd Wright

059
ANCIENT ARCHITECTURE #2

1. Which order of architecture is believed to have developed directly from wooden buildings?

a) Ionic
b) Tuscan
c) Corinthian
d) Doric

2. The capital of the Corinthian order is decorated with which type of leaves?

a) Shamrock
b) Olive
c) Oak
d) Acanthus

3. Who is the author of "De architetura", which became the standard text on classical architecture?

a) Filarete
b) Vitruvius
c) Leon Battista Alberti
d) Isidore of Miletus

4. What is the architectural style of Parthenon?

a) Doric
b) Ionic
c) Corinthian
d) none of them

5. Which of these temples is one of the Seven Wonders of the Ancient World?

a) The temple of Hephaestus
b) The temple of Hera
c) The temple of Apollo
d) The temple of Artemis

6. What is the oldest structure in Egypt?

a) Great Pyramid of Giza
b) Karnak Temple
c) Pyramid of Djoser
d) Luxor Temple

7. Which of these materials was used most in ancient Egypt?

a) Stone
b) Bricks
c) Clay
d) Wood

8. Herculaneum was an ancient town destroyed by which volcano?

a) Stromboli
b) Vesuvius
c) Lipari
d) Etna

9. What is a Stoa?

a) A portico/covered walkway
b) An administrative building
c) A temple
d) A special column

10. What was the old temple of Athena?

a) A Doric temple
b) A Ionic temple
c) An Archaic temple
d) A Corinthian temple

060
HISTORY OF ARCHITECTURE

1. Architecture in Egypt is largely characterized by which of the following styles?

a) Monumental style
b) Massiveness
c) Highly decorative style
d) Gothic style

2. What is the name of the ancient Roman construction technique which uses irregular shaped and uncut stones?

a) Opus caementium
b) Opus reticulatum
c) Opus quadratum
d) Opus incertum

3. How did the Romans create structures with huge spans?

a) By using arches
b) By large columns
c) By stone beams
d) By stone piles

4. Where did Gothic architecture originate?

a) Germany
b) Ireland
c) Spain
d) France

5. What is the shape of a Chinese pagoda in plan?

a) Square
b) Octagonal
c) Hexagonal
d) Rectangular

6. Which Greek term is the name given to an architectural column which takes the form of a standing female figure?

a) Astilar
b) Bartizan
c) Caryatid
d) Canephora

7. What capitol orders are combined in the Parthenon?

a) Doric, Ionic
b) Ionic, Corinthian
c) Tuscan, Corinthian
d) Corinthian, Ionic

8. Which architectural element was common in ancient Greek architecture?

a) Arches and vaults
b) Domes
c) Buttresses
d) Columns

9. Which materials were used to construct the pre-historic elephant hunter's camp, Terra Amata?

a) Branches and stones
b) Wood
c) Clay
d) Concrete

10. How tall is the Leshan Giant Buddha in China?

a) 51m (167ft)
b) 71m (233ft)
c) 91m (299ft)
d) 101m (331ft)

061
INDIAN ARCHITECTURE

1. The Pritzker Prize for 2018 was awarded to which Indian architect?

a) Charles Correa
b) Brinda Somaya
c) Balkrishna Doshi
d) Raj Rewal

2. Which of these styles is not seen in Indian temple architecture?

a) Mughal
b) Dravida
c) Vesara
d) Nagara

3. What is Mughal architecture best known for?

a) Gardens
b) Imperial mausoleums
c) Temples
d) Forts

4. What is the name of the largest Buddhist temple in the world located in India?

a) Mahabodhi temple
b) Borobudur temple
c) Wat Thai temple
d) Sarnath temple

5. What is a stupa mainly used for?

a) Meditation
b) Place of burial
c) Administrative building
d) Religious rituals

Answers to 060

6. How many minarets frame the tomb of Mumtaz Mahal, who was the inspiration for the Taj Mahal?

a) 2
b) 4
c) 6
d) 8

7. Who is known as the architect of modern India?

a) Jawaharlal Nehru
b) Nari Gandhi
c) Eulie Chowdhury
d) Anil Laul

8. What material is Sanchi Stupa, one of the oldest structures in India, made of?

a) Clay and send
b) Brick
c) Wood
d) Stone

9. How many buildings did Le Corbusier design in India?

a) 10
b) 14
c) 18
d) 20

10. Which of these historical monuments is used as a place of pilgrimage?

a) Brihadishwara Temple
b) Bahai Temple
c) Hawa Mahal
d) Harmandir Sahib

062
CHINESE ARCHITECTURE #1

1. When was the Zaozhou Stone Bridge built?

a) 800 years ago
b) 1000 years ago
c) 1200 years ago
d) 1400 years ago

2. Approximately, how old is the Leshan Giant Buddha, which lies east to Leshan City?

a) 1000 years
b) 1300 years
c) 1500 years
d) 2000 years

3. Dunhuang Mogao Caves, which are considered the oldest treasure of Buddhist art in the world, are also known as what?

a) Fifteen Buddha Caves
b) Hundred Buddha Caves
c) Thousand Buddha Caves
d) Million Buddha Caves

4. Which of these Chinese Wonders is sometimes called also "the Eighth Wonder of the World?

a) Terracotta Warriors
b) Great Wall of China
c) Baoxie Plank Road
d) Dunhuang Mogao Caves

5. Ancient Chinese architecture is mainly used which material?

a) Steel
b) Timber
c) Stones
d) Bricks

6. Approximately, how long is the Great Wall of China that we see today?

a) 2000km (1243 miles)
b) 4000km (2485 miles)
c) 6000km (3728 miles)
d) 8000km (12875 miles)

7. Chinese garden architecture can be traced back to the 16th century, what was its main purpose?

a) Meditation
b) Hunting
c) Relaxing
d) Other activities

8. Which of these important buildings in Chinese architecture houses the seat of the Dalai Lama?

a) Taipei 101
b) Yellow Crane Tower
c) Diwang Tower
d) Potala Palace

9. Who designed the Jin Mao Tower in China?

a) I. M. Pei
b) Norman Foster
c) Adrian Smith
d) Santiago Calatrava

10. Which of these architectural styles pursues the harmonious unity of humans and nature?

a) Taoism
b) Imperial Architecture
c) Buddhist Architecture
d) Garden Architecture

063
WHO SAID THIS?

1. "There are 360 degrees, so why stick to one?"

a) Daniel Libeskind
b) Zaha Hadid
c) Frank Gehry
d) Norman Foster

2. "Form ever follows function."

a) Louis Sullivan
b) Rem Koolhaas
c) Buckminster Fuller
d) Eileen Gray

3. "God is in the details."

a) Le Corbusier
b) Frank Lloyd Wright
c) Oscar Niemeyer
d) Mies van der Rohe

4. "Simplicity is the ultimate sophistication."

a) Walter Gropius
b) Leonardo da Vinci
c) I. M. Pei
d) Alvar Aalto

5. "An idea is salvation by imagination."

a) Tadao Ando
b) Frank Lloyd Wright
c) Richard Rogers
d) Jean Nouvel

6. "Architecture should speak of its time and place, but yearn for timelessness."

a) Eero Saarinen
b) Louis Kahn
c) Frank Gehry
d) Peter Zumthor

7. "The job of the architect today is to create beautiful buildings."

a) Bjarke Ingels
b) Richard Neutra
c) Louis Barragan
d) Philip Johnson

8. "To create, one must first question everything."

a) Eileen Gray
b) Santiago Calatrava
c) Marcel Breuer
d) Peter Eisenman

9. "I believe in God, only I spell it nature."

a) Frank Lloyd Wright
b) Toyo Ito
c) Steven Holl
d) Moshe Safdie

10. "Those who look for the laws of nature as a support for their new works collaborate with the creator."

a) Daniel Burnham
b) Alvaro Siza
c) Antoni Gaudi
d) Robert Venturi

064
TRAIN STATIONS

1. Which is the world's largest station by number of platforms?

a) Washington Union Station
b) Grand Central Terminal, NYC
c) Estación de Madrid Atocha, Madrid
d) St. Pancras International, London

2. Opened in 1864, Gare du Nord in Paris perfectly represents which style of architecture?

a) Beaux-Arts
b) Modern
c) Gothic
d) Classic

3. What was the first passenger railway station in the world?

a) Antwerp Central Station, Antwerp
b) Chicago Union Station, Chicago
c) Liverpool Road Railway station, Manchester
d) Gare du Nord, Paris

4. The Kenitra Train Station, in Morocco is designed to resemble which object?

a) A shell
b) A train
c) A house
d) A jewellery box

5. Which of these stations is also a UNESCO World Heritage Site?

a) Estación de Madrid Atocha, Spain
b) Chhatrapati Shivaji Terminus, Mumbai, India
c) Dunedin Railway Station, Dunedin, New Zealand
d) All of them

Answers to 063

1. b) Zaha Hadid	5. b) Frank Lloyd Wright	9. a) Frank Lloyd Wright
2. a) Louis Sullivan	6. c) Frank Gehry	10. c) Antoni Gaudi
3. d) Mies van der Rohe	7. d) Philip Johnson	
4. b) Leonardo da Vinci	8. a) Eileen Gray	

6. **Which of these famous museums is housed in a former railway station?**

a) Musee d'Orsay, Paris
b) Musee du Louvre, Paris
c) Museo del Prado, Madrid
d) The British Museum, London

7. **How many different types of marble were used in the Antwerpen-Centraal, Belgium?**

a) 5
b) 10
c) 15
d) 20

8. **Which London tube station was designed by Michael Hopkins in 1999 and shortlisted for the Stirling Prize?**

a) Paddington Station
b) Waterloo Station
c) Westminster Station
d) Charing Cross

9. **Which architect designed the Helsinki Central Station, Finland?**

a) Eero Saarinen
b) Eliel Saarinen
c) Herman Gesellius
d) Armas Lindgren

10. **How many previous stations existed on the current site that is Milano Centrale today?**

a) 0
b) 1
c) 2
d) 3

065

JAPANESE ARCHITECTURE

1. By which name are traditional houses in Japan known?

a) Minka
b) Shoji
c) Fusuma
d) Tokonoma

2. Which Japanese temple is considered the world's oldest surviving wooden structure?

a) Shitennoji Temple
b) Sanjusangendo Temple
c) Horyuji Temple
d) Kiyomizu-dera Temple

3. Which is often the dominant element in Japanese architecture?

a) Wall
b) Column
c) Arch
d) Roof

4. What is the tallest structure in Japan?

a) Tokyo Skytree
b) Rinku Gate Tower
c) Yokohama Landmark Tower
d) JR Central Office Tower

5. Which if these is the most recent architectural period in Japan?

a) Asuka and Nara architecture
b) Edo period
c) Heian period
d) Kamakura and Muromachi periods

Answers to 64

1. b) Grand Central Terminal
2. a) Beaux-Arts
3. c) Liverpool Road Railway station, Manchester
4. d) Jewellery box
5. b) Chhatrapati Shivaji Terminus, Mumbai, India
6. a) Musee d'Orsay
7. d) 20
8. c) Westminster Station
9. b) Eliel Saarinen
10. c) 2

6. How many Japanese architects had won the Pritzker Prize prior to Arata Isozaki winning in 2019?

a) 0
b) 1
c) 5
d) 7

7. What does the architectural style, Gassho-zukuri mean?

a) Raising hands
b) Praying hands
c) Clapping hands
d) Waving hands

8. How many different roof types would you find in Japanese architecture?

a) 1
b) 2
c) 3
d) 4

9. What is arguably the most famous building in Japan?

a) Imperial Palace
b) Hiroshima Peace Memorial Park
c) Historic Nara
d) Osaka Castle

10. Which of these Japanese buildings is considered one of the ugliest buildings in the World?

a) Tocho
b) Opera City Tower
c) Shiodome City Center
d) Aoyama Technical College

066
STONEHENGE

1. In which UK County is Stonehenge located?

   a) Somerset
   b) Wiltshire
   c) Berkshire
   d) Hampshire

2. How many stones make up the site at Stonehenge site?

   a) 40
   b) 64
   c) 101
   d) 83

3. How many different stone types were used to build Stonehenge?

   a) 1
   b) 2
   c) 3
   d) 4

4. It is believed that the construction of Stonehenge began around which year?

   a) 3000 BC
   b) 2500 BC
   c) 2000 BC
   d) 1500 BC

5. What is the composition of the stones at Stonehenge?

   a) Limestone & slate
   b) Sarsen sandstone & bluestone
   c) Argilite & anthracite
   d) Marble & granite

Answers to 065

1. a) Minka
2. c) Horyuji Temple
3. d) Roof
4. a) Tokyo Skytree

5. b) Edo period
6. d) 7
7. b) Praying hands
8. c) 3

9. a) Imperial Palace
10. d) Aoyama Technical
    College

6. How many construction phases was Stonehenge thought to have had?

a) 5
b) 4
c) 3
d) 2

7. The construction of Stonehenge took place in which period of time?

a) Lower palaeolithic age
b) Upper palaeolithic age
c) Mesolithic age
d) Neolithic age

8. Which two letters are used to name the rings of holes that were dug around the outside of the sarsen stone circle at Stonehenge?

a) R&S
b) X&W
c) Y&Z
d) A&B

9. What is the total weight of bluestones at Stonehenge?

a) 2-5 tons
b) 5-8 tons
c) 8-11 tons
d) 11-14 tons

10. What is the weight of sarsen stones at Stonehenge?

a) 5 tons
b) 15 tons
c) 20 tons
d) 25 tons

067
ISLAMIC ARCHITECTURE

1. What is the first structure that is considered to be Islamic architecture?

a) Dome of the Rock, Jerusalem
b) Taj Mahal, India
c) Sultan Amir Ahmad Bathhouse, Kashan
d) Chefchaouen, Morocco

2. Which of these features do minarets contain?

a) Domed tops
b) Staircases and balconies
c) Windows are not allowed
d) Cylindrical tapering shapes

3. Which of these features are not a characteristic of Islamic architecture?

a) Geometric patterns
b) Domes
c) Large glass windows
d) Pointed arches

4. Islamic architecture is mostly likely to be found in which type of building?

a) Civic buildings
b) Museums
c) Mosques
d) Secular buildings

5. Moorish architecture is a variation of Islamic architecture from which geographical region?

a) Turkey
b) North Africa and Spain
c) Eastern Asia
d) The Middle east

6. What type of building is the Alhambra in Spain?

a) Mosque
b) Palace
c) Courtyard
d) Tomb

7. What is the most common use of a minaret?

a) Call for a prayer
b) To deliver speeches to community
c) To indicate the location of the mosque
d) To point in the direction toward Mecca

8. The Blue Mosque is the nickname for which mosque in Istanbul?

a) The Hagia Sophia
b) The Haram Mosque
c) The Sultan Ahmed Mosque
d) The Ottoman Mosque

9. How many minarets does the Blue Mosque have?

a) 4
b) 5
c) 6
d) 7

10. Which architectural feature is common in Islamic courtyards?

a) Statues
b) Wind towers
c) Arches
d) Fountains

068
VICTORIAN ARCHITECTURE

1. Victorian architecture was prominent in Great Britian in which century?

a) 17th century
b) 18th century
c) 19th century
d) 20th century

2. Which of these countries was not affected by the spread of Victorian architecture?

a) Sri Lanka
b) Hong Kong
c) Australia
d) Morocco

3. Victorian architecture refers to buildings built during the reign of Queen Victoria, who reigned for how many years?

a) 43 years
b) 53 years
c) 63 years
d) 73 years

4. Which building material was most popular in Victorian architecture?

a) Bricks and mortar
b) Stone
c) Wood
d) Concrete

5. Who designed the Victorian, neo-gothic Manchester City town hall, completed in 1877?

a) John Ruskin
b) Charles Eastlake
c) Alfred Waterhouse
d) Frank Furness

6. Which of these UK buildings is considered as one of the most iconic iron and glass structures from the Victorian era?

a) Balmoral Castle
b) The Palm House, Kew Gardens
c) University of Liverpool
d) Royal Albert Hall

7. Which of the following is known as a pioneer of Victorian architecture?

a) Augustus Pugin
b) Richard Norman Shaw
c) William Butterfield
d) William Tite

8. St Paul's Cathedral in Melbourne, a Victorian style building, is designed by which architect?

a) Augustus Pugin
b) Richard Norman Shaw
c) William Butterfield
d) William Tite

9. How many styles preceeded the Victorian era that flourished in Australia (1840-1880)?

a) 10
b) 15
c) 20
d) 25

10. Victorian architecture was succeeded by which style?

a) Georgian architecture
b) Regency architecture
c) Edwardian architecture
d) Rococo architecture

069
MEDIEVAL ARCHITECTURE

1. Which of these types of buildings are included in Medieval architecture?

a) Religious buildings
b) Military buildings
c) Civil buildings
d) All of them

2. Which of these architectural styles are found in Medieval architecture?

a) Pre-Romanesque
b) Romanesque
c) Gothic
d) All of them

3. Which is arguably the most famous Medieval building in Europe?

a) Westminster Abbey
b) Airth Castle
c) Akershus Fortress
d) Buckfast Abbey

4. Durham Cathedral is considered one of the best examples of which architectural style?

a) Pre-Romanesque
b) Romanesque
c) Gothic
d) Classical architecture

5. Which of these famous buildings is sometimes referred to as the 'key to England'?

a) Tower of London
b) Warwick Castle
c) Dover Castle
d) Hedingham Castle

6. What are some of the surviving examples of military structures in medieval architecture?

a) Castles
b) Fortified walls
c) Both of them
d) None of them

7. Within a church what is the apse?

a) Semicircular niche at the east end
b) A walkway
c) Open entrance hall
d) A part of building wall, pierced with windows

8. Which of these cathedrals cannot be categorised as Medieval architecture?

a) Lincoln Cathedral
b) York Minster Cathedral
c) Ely Cathedral
d) Basilica of the Fourteen Holy Helpers

9. The Amiens Cathedral, a UNESCO world heritage site, was built in which century?

a) 12th century
b) 13th century
c) 14th century
d) 15th century

10. How many towers does Durham Cathedral have?

a) 1
b) 2
c) 3
d) 4

070
RENAISSANCE ARCHITECTURE

1. In Renaissance architecture, the plans are characterized by which symmetrical shape?

a) Oval
b) Square
c) Triangle
d) Circular

2. Who is considered to be the first to developed the Renaissance architecture?

a) Vitruvius
b) Andrea Palladio
c) Michelangelo
d) Filippo Brunelleschi

3. Who was appointed the architect of St. Peter's Basilica in the Vatican City, in 1546?

a) Michelangelo
b) Raphael
c) Donato Bramante
d) Leonardo da Vinci

4. Which of these famous architects does not belong in the Renaissance period?

a) Giorgo Vasari
b) Donato Bramante
c) Ictinus
d) Jacopo Sansovino

5. Who proposed the Greek-cross plan in Renaissance architecture?

a) Leon Battista Alberti
b) Brunelleschi
c) Sebastiano Serlio
d) Giulliano da Sangallo

1. d) All of them

2. d) All of them

3. a) Westminster Abbey

4. b) Romanesque

5. c) Dover Castle

6. c) Both of them

7. a) Semicircular niche at
   the east end

8. d) Basilica of the Fourteen
   Holy Helpers

9. b) 13th century

10. c) 3

6. **Roman Renaissance architects derived their main designs and inspirations from which classical models?**

a) Greek
b) Romans
c) None of them
d) Both of them

7. **Which architect introduced the High Renaissance style?**

a) Michelangelo
b) Donato Bramante
c) Leonardo da Vinci
d) Filippo Brunelleschi

8. **Which of these styles did the Renaissance succeed in France?**

a) Classical
b) Neoclassical
c) Gothic
d) Classicism

9. **Which architect is well known for his theory: firmitas (strength), utilitas (functionality), and venustas (beauty)?**

a) Raphael
b) Vitruvius
c) Michelangelo
d) Leonardo da Vinci

10. **Who designed the Palazzo Ducale di Urbino in Italy?**

a) Luciano Laurana
b) Vignola
c) Michele Sanmicheli
d) Antonio Contini

071
BAROQUE ARCHITECTURE

1. In which period was Baroque architecture founded?

a) 1465-1680
b) 1584-1750
c) 1620-1840
d) 1685-1896

2. In which countries was the high Baroque style developed?

a) France and Germany
b) Italy and Germany
c) France and Italy
d) Germany and Spain

3. How many statues of saints are there in St. Peter's Square and its colonnades?

a) 140
b) 150
c) 160
d) 170

4. Who was the architect of the Palace of Versailles and Les Invalides?

a) Jules Hardouin-Mansart
b) Luigi Vanvitelli
c) Alonso Cano
d) Jacob van Campen

5. What is 'High Baroque' style otherwise known as?

a) Romanesque
b) Rococo
c) Neoclassical
d) Empire Style

1. b) Square

2. d) Filippo Brunelleschi

3. a) Michelangelo

4. c) Ictinus

5. a) Leon Battista Alberti

6. d) Both of them

7. b) Donato Bramante

8. c) Gothic

9. b) Vitruvius

10. a) Luciano Laurana

6. **The Zacatecas Cathedral is located in which country?**

a) Peru
b) Argentina
c) Brazil
d) Mexico

7. **What does baroque mean?**

a) Ornate
b) Classical
c) Irregularly shaped
d) Regularly shaped

8. **What are the major characteristics of baroque style?**

a) Drama & vitality
b) Movement & tension
c) Emotional exuberance
d) All of them

9. **Baroque art was initiated in reaction to which style of the late Renaissance?**

a) Minimalist
b) Classical
c) Mannerist
d) Neoclassical

10. **Who was the leading Baroque sculptor and architect?**

a) Balthasar Neumann
b) Bernini
c) Louis Le Vau
d) Andrea Pozzo

072
MINIMALIST ARCHITECTURE

1. Minimalist architecture is based on which of the following?

a) The absence of architecture
b) The essence of architecture
c) The historical aspect of architecture
d) The infinite possibilities of architecture

2. Which of the following is not considered as important in minimalist architecture?

a) Space
b) Light
c) Materials
d) Ornamentation

3. Minimalist architecture emerged from which styles?

a) De Stijl & Bauhaus
b) Art Deco & Moderne
c) Brutalism & Contextualism
d) Art Deco & Bauhaus

4. Minimalist architecture is inspired by which of the following philosophies?

a) Buddhism
b) Taoism
c) Zen
d) Shinto

5. Which of these minimalist architects has been awarded a Pritzker Prize?

a) Peter Zumthor
b) Tadao Ando
c) Neither
d) Both of them

6. In which decade was minimalist architecture first conceived?

a) 1920s
b) 1930s
c) 1940s
d) 1950s

7. Which of these statements is the motto of minimalist designers?

a) Recognizing the need is the primary condition for design
b) Form ever follows function
c) Less is more
d) A brilliant design will always benefit from the input of others

8. The traditional style of which country has influenced minimalist design most significantly?

a) Japan
b) Chinese
c) Indian
d) German

9. Which of the following are considered influencers of minimalist design?

a) Dieter Rams
b) Buckminster Fuller
c) Mies van der Rohe
d) All of them

10. Which of these architects emphasize nothingness and empty space to show the elegance of simplicity?

a) Frank Lloyd Wright
b) Tadao Ando
c) Frank Gehry
d) Zaha Hadid

073
UGLY ARCHITECTURE

1. Who designed Boston City Hall?

a) Laurie Baker
b) Kallmann & McKinnell
c) Ole Scheeren
d) Adolf Loos

2. Who designed North Korea's Ryugyong Hotel, also called the 'Hotel of Doom'?

a) Michael Graves
b) Nari Gandhi
c) Cesar Pelli
d) Baikdoosan Architects & Engineers

3. Who designed the Kaden Tower in Louisville, Kentucky?

a) William Wesley Peters
b) Mitchel Guirgola
c) Edward Barnes
d) Jose Luis Sert

4. Who designed Simmons Hall at the Massachusetts Institute of Technology?

a) Charles Correa
b) Charles Eames
c) Steven Holl
d) Konstantin Melnikov

5. Who designed Lincoln Plaza, London?

a) James Sterling
b) Christian de Portzamparc
c) SOM
d) BUJ Architects

6. **Who designed 'The Rock', Wellington's International Airport Terminal in New Zealand?**

a) Carlo Rossi
b) Studio Pacific Architecture
c) Hafeez Contractor
d) Bartolomeo Rastrelli

7. **Who designed The Elephant Building in Bangkok, Thailand?**

a) Sumset Jumsai
b) Charles Cameron
c) Buckminster Fuller
d) Fran Silvestre

8. **Who designed the Renmin Ribao Building in Beijing, China?**

a) Robert Venturi
b) Karl Blank
c) Zhou Qi
d) Patricia Urquiola

9. **Who designed The Fang Yuan Building in China?**

a) Rafael Moneo
b) C. Y. Lee
c) Ricardo Bofill
d) Enric Miralles

10. **Who designed the National Library in Minsk, Belarus?**

a) Dieter Rams
b) Vasili Bazhenov
c) Nicholas Benois
d) Vinogradov & Kramarenko

074
PYRAMIDS OF EGYPT

1. Which material was used to build the pyramids of Egypt?

a) Masonry
b) Concrete
c) Iron
d) All of them

2. How many pyramids were discovered in Egypt?

a) 128
b) 138
c) 148
d) 158

3. What was the function of a pyramid?

a) Tomb
b) Religious place
c) Palace
d) Temple

4. Which Pharaoh built the first pyramid?

a) Ramses
b) Ptolemy
c) Djoser
d) Khufu

5. What was the largest pyramid built by the ancient Egyptians?

a) The Red Pyramid of Snofru
b) The Pyramid of MenKaure
c) The Pyramid of Djoser
d) The Great Pyramid of Giza

6. When was the Pyramid of Giza built?

a) 5500 years ago
b) 4500 years ago
c) 3500 years ago
d) 2500 years ago

7. The great pyramids maintain a constant inside temperature of how many degrees?

a) 10°C (50°F)
b) 15°C (59°F)
c) 20°C (68°F)
d) 25°C (77°F)

8. Who is the famous architect of the pyramids?

a) Ineni
b) Senemut
c) Hemiunu
d) Imhotep

9. What specific location do all Egyptian pyramids have in common?

a) West side of the Nile River
b) East side of the Nile River
c) Outside Cairo
d) On the coast of the Red Sea

10. How much does one piece of stone in the Great Pyramid of Giza weigh?

a) 2.5 - 15 tons
b) 5 -1 0 tons
c) 7.5 - 20 tons
d) 12.5 - 20 tons

075
MOSQUES

1. Which of these features would you find in a mosque?

a) Mihrab
b) Minaret
c) Sahn
d) All of them

2. What is the dome of a mosque called?

a) Qubba
b) Mihrab
c) Minbar
d) Kaaba

3. Which is the oldest mosque in the world?

a) Al-Aqsa Mosque, Jerusalem
b) The Quba Mosque, Saudi Arabia
c) The Blue Mosque, Istanbul
d) Mosques of the Companions, Sudan

4. Where is Kaaba, the focal point of Islamic rituals also known as 'The House of God', located?

a) Al-Nabawi Mosque
b) Dome of the Rock
c) Al-Haram Mosque
d) Al-Aqsa Mosque

5. What is a Jama Masjid?

a) Friday mosque
b) Everyone's mosque
c) Little mosque
d) Old mosque

6. Djamaa el Djazaïr has the tallest minaret in the world. How tall is it?

a) 235m (771ft)
b) 245m (804ft)
c) 255m (837ft)
d) 265m (869ft)

7. In which century was the Sultan Ahmed Mosque built?

a) 15th century
b) 16th century
c) 17th century
d) 18th century

8. Which of the following architects is most famous for designing mosques?

a) Vedat Dalokay
b) Mimar Sinan
c) Marina Tabassum
d) Sedefkar Mehmed Agha

9. What is a mihrab?

a) A tribune raised upon columns from which the Quran is recited
b) The pulpit from which the Friday sermon is delivered
c) A place for pilgrimage
d) A semicircular niche in the wall that indicates the direction of the Kaaba

10. Which is the only country in Europe that does not have any mosques?

a) Slovakia
b) France
c) Czech Republic
d) Croatia

076
PARLIAMENTARY BUILDINGS

1. Which of the following is considered to be the most famous Parliamentary building in Europe?

a) Binnenhof, Netherlands
b) The Palace of Parliament, Romania
c) Hungarian Parliament Building
d) Austrian Parliament Building

2. In which architectural style was Westminster Palace built?

a) Baroque
b) Gothic Revival
c) Contemporary
d) Rustic

3. According to Guinness World Records, which is the heaviest Parliament building in the world?

a) The Palace of Parliament, Bucharest
b) Parliament House, Canberra
c) Capitol Building, US
d) The Reichstag, Germany

4. Which is the oldest parliamentary building in the world that is still in use today?

a) Palace of Westminster, UK
b) Parliament Building, Northern Ireland
c) Parliament House, Finland
d) Binnenhof, Netherlands

5. The brown roof of the Beehive, New Zealand's Parliamentary building, is constructed from which material?

a) Iron
b) Copper
c) Gold
d) Wood

6. What is the statue at the top of the dome of The Capitol Building, Washington DC called?

a) The Statue of Liberty
b) The Statue of Equality
c) The Statue of Freedom
d) The Statue of Hope

7. The Palace of the National Congress in Brazil, was designed by which architect?

a) Oscar Niemeyer
b) Le Corbusier
c) Lucio Costa
d) Roberto Marx

8. National Diet Building is the name of the parliamentary building in which country?

a) China
b) India
c) Canada
d) Japan

9. What is the architectural style of the parliamentary building in the Czech Republic?

a) Rococo
b) Baroque
c) Modern
d) Gothic

10. What is the Seat of Parliament in Trinidad and Tobago called?

a) The Green House
b) The White House
c) The Red House
d) The Blue House

077
MODERN ARCHITECTURE #2

1. Which architectural movement is characterized by an absence of harmony, continuity and symmetry?

a) Googie architecture
b) Art Deco
c) High-tech
d) Deconstructivism

2. What is the primary material used in Brutalist architecture?

a) Steel
b) Concrete
c) Sedum
d) Timber

3. Which of these is not a dominant style in Modern architecture?

a) International style
b) Constructivist
c) Brutalist
d) Expressionist

4. Einstein Tower in Potsdam, Germany is an iconic building in which architectural style?

a) International style
b) Constructivist
c) Brutalist
d) Expressionist

5. Which of these forms of modern architecture flourished in the Soviet Union in 1920s and 1930s?

a) International style
b) Constructivist
c) Brutalist
d) Expressionist

6. Which of these famous buildings is not high-tech architecture?

a) Trellick Tower, London
b) Lloyd's Building, London
c) Allianz Arena, Munich
d) Center Pompidou, Paris

7. Which style is considered to be indifferent to location, site and climate and is supposed to be universally applicable?

a) International style
b) De Stijl
c) Cubism
d) Art Deco

8. Villa Savoye is an icon of which architectural style?

a) International style
b) Bauhaus
c) Minimalism
d) Mid-century modern

9. The harmony between human habitation and the natural world is best promoted in which style?

a) Art Nouveau
b) Neo-Expressionism
c) Organic architecture
d) Functionalism

10. Which style emerged as a reaction against the austerity, formality and lack of variety of modern architecture?

a) Art Deco
b) De Stijl
c) High-tech
d) Post modern

078
PAGODAS

1. What is the shape of the base of a pagoda?

a) Circle
b) Square
c) Triangle
d) Oval

2. Which of these famous pagodas is one of the only pagodas to be built with an even number of levels?

a) Toji Pagoda, Japan
b) Kew Gardens Pagoda, UK
c) Yellow Crane Pagoda, China
d) The Pagoda on Skyline Drive, U.S

3. Which ancient Indian building type is the predecessors of pagodas?

a) Sorin
b) Temple
c) Stupa
d) Shrine

4. What do the five levels of Japanese pagodas symbolize?

a) Hardness, moistness, heat, mobility, stillness
b) Rock, sea, smoke, weather, sky
c) Earth, water, fire, wind, space
d) Flower, enlightenment, bodhisattvas, grave, deities

5. Which of these countries is most famous for its Pagodas?

a) South Africa
b) Myanmar (Burma)
c) USA
d) France

6. Which element crowns the main stupa of the Shwedagon Pagoda?

a) The Crown Umbrella
b) The Crown Spire
c) The Brick Umbrella
d) The King's Spire

7. Which material was used to cover the structure of the main stupa of the Shwedagon Temple?

a) Marble
b) Bronze
c) Silver
d) Gold

8. How many sides does a Chinese pagoda usually have?

a) 2
b) 3
c) 4
d) 5

9. What did a pagoda initially symbolize?

a) A sacred mountain
b) A house of God
c) A tower
d) A cloud

10. The first pagoda appeared in China and was built by Emperor Ming to spread the Buddha's teachings. In which year was it built?

a) 28 AD
b) 68 AD
c) 100 AD
d) 200 AD

079
SANTIAGO CALATRAVA

1. Which architectural style did Calatrava have?

a) High-tech
b) Neoclassical
c) Post-modern
d) All of them

2. In which university did Calatrava study?

a) ETH Zurich
b) Polytechnic University of Valencia
c) Delft University of Technology
d) All of them

3. Which of these buildings is not designed by Calatrava?

a) Olympic Athletic Center of Athens "Spiros Louis"
b) Auditorio de Tenerife Adán Martín
c) Liège-Guillemins Railway Station
d) Nemo Science Center in Amsterdam

4. Which is regarded as the most famous project of Calatrava?

a) Milwaukee Art Museum, Milwaukee
b) City of Arts and Sciences, Valencia
c) Turning Tors Tower, Malmo
d) The Margaret Hunt Hill Bridge, Dallas

5. What type of structures is Calatrava most known for?

a) His bridges supported by single leaning pylons
b) His high towers
c) His famous residential buildings and villas
d) All of them

Answers to 078

1. b) Square

2. b) Kew Gardens Pagoda, UK

3. c) Stupa

4. c) Earth, water, fire, wind, space

5. b) Myanmar (Burma)

6. a) The Crown Umbrella

7. d) Gold

8. c) 4

9. a) A sacred mountain

10. b) 68 AD

6. In 1984, Calatrava designed the first of the bridge projects that established his international reputation. What was this project?

a) The Constitution Bridge in Venice
b) he Margaret Hunt Hill Bridge, Dallas
c) The Bach de Roda Bridge in Barcelona
d) The Alamillo Bridge in Seville.

7. As well as architecture, which of these professions does Calatrava have?

a) Sculptor
b) Structural Engineer
c) Painter
d) All of them

8. What did Calatrava receive a bad name for?

a) For making his construction works extremely expensive
b) For taking a very long time for a project
c) For not using ecological materials
d) All of them

9. How many projects has Calatrava designed so far?

a) 36
b) 48
c) 64
d) 75

10. How long is the Constitution Bridge, considered the most famous bridge designed by Calatrava?

a) 58m (190ft)
b) 68m (223ft)
c) 78m (256ft)
d) 88m (289ft)

080
MUSEUMS

1. Which city has the greatest number of museums in the world (144 museums)?

a) New York City
b) Amsterdam
c) Paris
d) Rome

2. Which of the following is considered to be the most famous museum in the world?

a) Tate Modern, London
b) MOMA, NYC
c) Musée du Louvre, Paris
d) National Palace Museum, Taipei

3. How many ancient Egyptian artefacts does the Museum of Egyptian Antiquities in Cairo, one of the largest museums in North Africa, house?

a) 120 000
b) 150 000
c) 200 000
d) 250 000

4. Who was the architect of the San Francisco Museum of Modern Art (SFMOMA)?

a) Calatrava
b) Frank Gehry
c) Frank Lloyd Wright
d) Mario Botta

5. Which was the first museum in the world to open its doors to the public in 1734?

a) The Capitoline Museums, Rome
b) Belvedere Palace, Vienna
c) Musée du Louvre, Paris
d) Royal Armouries, London

6. Known as the "Picasso of concrete," who is the architect that designed the Niterói Contemporary Art Museum, in Rio de Janeiro?

a) Walter Gropius
b) Oscar Niemeyer
c) Zaha Hadid
d) Renzo Piano

7. Which of these museums was designed by Polish-American architect Daniel Libeskind?

a) Guggenheim Museum, Bilbao
b) Tate Modern, London
c) The Denver Art Museum, Denver
d) Belvedere Palace, Vienna

8. Which of these museums had once been a railway station?

a) Musée D'Orsay, Paris
b) The Art Institute of Chicago
c) Museo Larco in Lima
d) State Hermitage Museum in St. Petersburg

9. In which year did Michelangelo's David join the museum Galleria dell'Accademia in Florence?

a) 1796
b) 1820
c) 1854
d) 1873

10. Which of these museums is the World Holocaust Remembrance Center?

a) U.S Holocaust Memorial Museum
b) Yad Vashem Holocaust Memorial, Jerusalem
c) Sydney Jewish Museum
d) Jewish Museum, London

081
OPERA HOUSES

1. Which of these buildings is a UNESCO World Heritage site?

a) Sydney Opera House
b) Copenhagen Opera House
c) Tatri i Operas dhe Baletit, Albania
d) Hungarian State Opera

2. Which of these opera houses is named after the man who designed it?

a) Bolshoi Theatre
b) Teatro di San Carlo
c) Lincoln Center
d) Palais Garnier

3. What is the architectural style of the Vienna State Opera House?

a) Gothic
b) Renaissance Revival
c) Baroque
d) Modern

4. Which of these buildings is well known for its eclectic architecture?

a) Teatro Colón, Buenos Aires
b) La Scala Opera House, Milan
c) Copenhagen Opera House
d) all of them

5. In which city is the Mariinsky Theatre located?

a) Prague, Czech Republic
b) Budapest, Hungary
c) Bucharest, Romania
d) St Petersburg, Russia

6. **Who wass the architect of the Guangzhou Opera House in China?**

a) Frank Lloyd Wright
b) Renzo Piano
c) Zaha Hadid
d) Rem Koolhaas

7. **How many tiles cover the "sails" of the Sydney Opera House structure?**

a) 1.056 million
b) 1.566 million
c) 2.056 million
d) 2.566 million

8. **Which is the oldest opera house in Italy?**

a) Teatro La Fenice, Venice
b) Teatro di San Carlo, Naples
c) Teatro Massimo, Palermo
d) Teatro alla Scala, Milan

9. **How old is the Bolshoi Theatre, Moscow?**

a) 130 years old
b) 156 years old
c) 199 years old
d) 207 years old

10. **Which city in Europe has the most opera houses?**

a) Berlin
b) Moscow
c) Vienna
d) Paris

082
THE NEW SEVEN WONDERS OF THE WORLD

1. When were the new seven wonders of the world announced?

a) July 2007
b) August 2008
c) November 2009
d) December 2010

2. How many regions of China does The Great Wall span across?

a) 5
b) 10
c) 15
d) 20

3. Which of the New Seven Wonders is the newest and opened in 1931?

a) Taj Mahal
b) Colosseum
c) Christ The Redeemer
d) Petra

4. Where is Chichen Itza located?

a) Mexico
b) Peru
c) Brazil
d) Colombia

5. What is the Taj Mahal?

a) A Castle
b) A Mausoleum
c) A Garden
d) A Temple

6. At which site would you find The Temple of the Sun, The Room of the Three Windows and Intihuatana?

a) Machu Picchu
b) Chichen Itza
c) Great Wall of China
d) Taj Mahal

7. How many Royal Tombs are there at the archaeological site of Petra?

a) 200
b) 600
c) 800
d) 1200

8. What material is the Brazilian Christ the Redeemer statue made of?

a) Marble
b) Soapstone
c) Alabaster
d) Granite

9. Which of these sites was rediscovered in 1911 by Hiram Bingham?

a) Colosseum
b) Great Wall of China
c) Taj Mahal
d) Machu Picchu

10. Which of these is not a New Wonder of the World?

a) Statue of Liberty
b) Machu Picchu
c) Petra
d) Colosseum

083
LUDWIG MIES VAN DER ROHE

1. Ludwig Mies van der Rohe is one of the pioneers of which style of architecture?

a) Classic architecture
b) Modernist architecture
c) Post modern architecture
d) Brutalist architecture

2. Which of these buildings is considered as Mies van der Rohe's masterpiece?

a) Barcelona Pavilion, Spain
b) Urbif House, Germany
c) IBM Building, Chicago
d) Crown Hall, Chicago

3. Which building is considered as Mies' first truly modern house?

a) Tugendhat House, Brno, Czech Republic
b) Farnsworth House, Illinois
c) Crown Hall, Chicago
d) None of them

4. In which year did Mies van der Rohe become director of the Bauhaus?

a) 1920
b) 1930
c) 1940
d) 1950

5. Which of these materials did Mies van der Rohe use in the Martin Luther King Jr. Memorial Library?

a) Steel
b) Brick
c) Glass
d) All of them

6. Which of these features is unique to the Lemke House, designed by Mies in Berlin?

a) The courtyard
b) The windows
c) The colours
d) The terrace

7. What is the height of The Seagram Building in New York?

a) 124m (407ft)
b) 138m (453ft)
c) 157m (515ft)
d) 167m (548ft)

8. What is the name of the project, conceived as a prototype intended for mass housing production?

a) 50 x 50 feet House
b) 60 x 60 feet House
c) 70 x 70 feet House
d) 80 x 80 feet House

9. In which year did Ludwig Mies van der Rohe die?

a) 1957
b) 1969
c) 1990
d) 1998

10. What was Ludwig Mies van der Rohe last work?

a) Martin Luther King Jr. Memorial Library, Washington D.C
b) Farnsworth House, Chicago
c) Urbif House, Germany
d) New National Gallery of Berlin

084

IRANIAN ARCHITECTURE

1. The traditional architecture of Iran can be categorized into how many styles?

a) 2
b) 4
c) 6
d) 8

2. What is the nickname of Nasir Al-Mulk Mosque in Shiraz?

a) Blue Mosque
b) Red Mosque
c) Pink Mosque
d) Green Mosque

3. Which material covers the exterior side of Sheikh Lotfollah mosque dome?

a) Silver
b) Tiles
c) Timber
d) Glass

4. The ancient city of Persepolis was the ceremonial capital of which Empire?

a) Achaemenid Empire
b) Afsharid Empire
c) Ghaznavid Empire
d) Safavid Empire

5. Which of these buildings is considered the largest adobe building in the world?

a) Yakhcha, Yazd
b) Tower of Silence, Yazd
c) Khaju Bridge, Isfahan
d) Arg-e Bam, Kerman

6. How many arches does the 133m (436ft) long Khaju Bridge in Isfahan have?

a) 17
b) 20
c) 23
d) 26

7. What is the Naqsh-e Rajab, located about 12km (7.5 miles) north-west of Persepolis?

a) Necropolis
b) Acropolis
c) Amphitheatre
d) None of them

8. How many UNESCO world heritage sites are located within Iran?

a) 10
b) 20
c) 30
d) 40

9. The Tomb of Daniel in Susa is famous for which shape of dome?

a) Spherical
b) Semispherical
c) Onion
d) Conical

10. By 400 BC, Persian engineers had mastered the technique of storing ice which was brought in during the winter and stored in the ice-pit, within which type of building?

a) Badgir
b) Barracks
c) Yakhchal
d) Caravanserai

085
BARCELONA

1. Which type of architecture is most common in Barcelona?

a) Catalan Gothic
b) Modernism
c) Both of them
d) None of them

2. Who is considered to be "the architect of Barcelona"?

a) Santiago Calatrava
b) Rafael Moneo
c) Ricardo Bofill
d) Antoni Gaudi

3. How many monumental façades, each connected to a moment in life of Christ, does Sagrada Familia have?

a) 1
b) 2
c) 3
d) 4

4. The Arc de Triomf in Barcelona was built by Josep Vilaseca i Casanovas to serve as the main entrance to which green space?

a) Parc de la Ciutadella
b) Parc Guell
c) Jardin de Laribal
d) Parc de Cervantes

5. The Barcelona Pavilion was designed by which architect?

a) Antoni Gaudi
b) Santiago Calatrava
c) Mies van der Rohe
d) Ricardo Bofill

6. Which is the tallest building in Barcelona?

a) Torre Agbar
b) Torre Mapfre
c) Habitat Sky
d) Torre Puig

7. The Agbar Tower is made up of concentric concrete oval cylinders which do not come in contact with each other. How many cylinders are there?

a) 5
b) 2
c) 3
d) 4

8. How many spires were there in the original design of Sagrada Familia?

a) 12
b) 14
c) 16
d) 18

9. Which of these buildings is considered an architectural jewel of Catalan Art Nouveau, listed as a World Heritage Site by UNESCO?

a) The Palau de la Música Catalana
b) Torre Mare Nostrum
c) Casa Milla
d) Casa Batllo

10. Where in Barcelona is the Cascada Fountain located?

a) Parc del Laberint d'Horta
b) Parc de Montjuic
c) Parc de la Ciutadella
d) Jardin Botanico de Barcelona

086

MEDITERRANEAN ARCHITECTURE

1. Where did Mediterranean architecture first become a trend?

a) Europe
b) South America
c) North America
d) Asia

2. Who was the 'key' architect in the development of the Mediterranean style?

a) Addison Mizner
b) Bertram Goodhue
c) Wallace Harrison
d) George Washington Smith

3. Which of these is not a feature of Mediterranean architecture?

a) Red colour roofing tiles
b) Combination of limestone flooring with terracotta
c) Wooden roof
d) Stucco walls

4. When did Mediterranean architecture become popular?

a) 1920s
b) 1940s
c) 1960s
d) 2000s

5. Which of these buildings is not an example of Mediterranean architecture?

a) Ambassador Hotel, L.A
b) Casa Vicens, Spain
c) Atalaya Castle, South Carolina
d) Cà d'Zan, Florida

6. Who was the architect of the Sunrise Theatre, also known as the Sunrise Building, one of the best examples of Mediterranean Revival architecture?

a) Ralph Adams Cram
b) Vincent Ferrer
c) Charles William Dickey
d) John N. Sherwood

7. The Highland Park Masonic Temple, also known as The Mason Building or The Highlands, is a historic brick building in L.A. How many stories does it have?

a) 3
b) 7
c) 10
d) 12

8. Which of these City Hall buildings was built in a Mediterranean revival style with a Corinthian colonnade?

a) Boston City Hall
b) Coral Gabels City Hall
c) Dallas City Hall
d) All of them

9. Which colours would you find on the walls in a Mediterranean style house?

a) Pastel colours
b) Light colours
c) Dark colours
d) White and blue

10. How many styles of Mediterranean homes are there?

a) 1
b) 2
c) 3
d) 4

087
ZAHA HADID

1. Where was Zaha Hadid born?

a) United Kingdom
b) Iraq
c) Iran
d) Germany

2. In which year did Zaha Hadid win the Pritzker prize?

a) 1994
b) 1998
c) 2004
d) 2010

3. What title was Zaha Hadid awarded in the Queen's 2012 birthday honours for services to Architecture?

a) Dame
b) Baroness
c) Duchess
d) Countess

4. Apart from the Pritzker Prize, which of these prizes did Zaha Hadid win?

a) Gold Medal Architectural Design
b) Thomas Jeferson Medal in Architecture
c) Erich Schelling Architecture Award
d) All of them

5. The Al Wakrah Stadium designed for the FIFA World Cup in Qatar 2022, was inspired by which of the following?

a) The water in motion
b) A fishing boat
c) A shell
d) A ball

6. How many projects did Zaha Hadid design?

a) Almost 500
b) Almost 800
c) Almost 1000
d) Almost 1300

7. Which of Hadid's projects was canceled just 3 days after being the winning entry of an international competition?

a) The Millenium Project
b) MAXXI Museum
c) Messner Mountain Museum
d) Heydar Aliyev Center

8. What did Zaha Hadid study before architecture?

a) Physics
b) Mathematics
c) Literature
d) Philosophy

9. Which of these projects was completed soon after her death?

a) The Salermo Maritime Terminal, Italy
b) Issam Fares Institute, Beirut, Lebanon
c) Rosenthal Center for Contemporary Art, Cincinnati, Ohio
d) Maggie's Centers at the Victoria Hospital, UK

10. In what year did Zaha Hadid die?

a) 2000
b) 2006
c) 2010
d) 2016

088
MOROCCAN ARCHITECTURE

1. In which year was Moroccan architecture first recorded?

   a) 210 BC
   b) 110 BC
   c) 110 AD
   d) 210AD

2. Which material was mostly used in early Moroccan buildings?

   a) Stone
   b) Tiles
   c) Mud bricks
   d) All of them

3. What is a traditional Moroccan house called?

   a) A riad
   b) An andaruni
   c) A howz
   d) A zenana

4. The Koutoubia Mosque in Djemaa el-Fna is the second mosque of this name built by 'Abd al-Mu'min after the first was destroyed. Why was this?

   a) As it was an inappropriate building
   b) As it was wrongly oriented
   c) After a fire
   d) After an earthquake hit the country

5. The "Bank of Africa Tower", scheduled to be finished by the end of May 2022 is designed to be the tallest skyscraper in Africa. What is it's final height?

   a) 100m (328ft)
   b) 150m (492ft)
   c) 200m (656ft)
   d) 250m (820ft)

6. In which city is the famous Bahia Palace located?

a) Marrakesh
b) Rabat
c) Fez
d) Casablanca

7. What is the Hassan Tower in Morocco?

a) The tallest tower in Morocco
b) A residential tower
c) The minaret of an incomplete mosque
d) An office building

8. Which is the only round minaret in Morocco?

a) Minaret of Grand Mosque, Chefchaouen
b) Minaret of Moulay Idriss Zerhoun Mosque
c) Minaret of Ahl Fas Mosque
d) None of them

9. Around which decade the was El Badi Palace constructed?

a) 1570s
b) 1600s
c) 1680s
d) 1740s

10. Located in Morocco, what is the largest mosque in Africa?

a) Great Mosque of Taza
b) Al-Fath Mosque
c) Ad-Doha Mosque
d) The Hassan II Mosque

089

THE COLOSSEUM

1. Which of the following is an alternative name for the Colosseum in Rome?

a) The Caesareum Amphitheatre
b) The Flavian Amphitheatre
c) The Nero Amphitheatre
d) The Vespasian Amphithetre

2. What is the shape of The Colosseum?

a) Oval
b) Circular
c) Semi-circular
d) Square

3. When was The Colosseum built?

a) 60-50 BC
b) 10-20 AD
c) 30-40 AD
d) 70-80 AD

4. The arcades of The Colosseum, are framed by half-columns of which order?

a) Ionic
b) Doric
c) Corinthian
d) All of them

5. How long is The Colosseum in plan?

a) 69m (226ft)
b) 129m (423ft)
c) 189m (620ft)
d) 249m (817ft)

6. How wide is The Colosseum in plan?

a) 136m (446ft)
b) 156m (512ft)
c) 176m (577ft)
d) 196m (643ft)

7. What is the height of the outer wall of The Colosseum?

a) 48m (157ft)
b) 5m (16ft)
c) 75m (246ft)
d) 123m (404ft)

8. How many people could The Colosseum accommodate according to the Codex Calendar of 354AD?

a) 50 000
b) 65 000
c) 79 000
d) 87 000

9. How many entrances did The Colosseum have at the ground level?

a) 10
b) 40
c) 80
d) 100

10. Which of the main/axial entrances was reserved for the Roman Emperor?

a) Northern
b) Southern
c) Western
d) Eastern

090
STRANGE STRUCTURES

1. Which of these strange structures related to sustainability did architect Mike Reynolds design?

a) Eco-home
b) Earthship
c) Earthtrack
d) None of them

2. The Green Wall of the Sahara is an ambitious plan that is trying to create a literal wall of greenery at the edge of the Sahara Desert. How many different countries does this project involve?

a) 15
b) 18
c) 21
d) 23

3. Which architect invented the word "arcology"?

a) Paolo Soleri
b) Renzo Piano
c) John Lautner
d) Frank Lloyd Wright

4. Arcology is a combination of which words?

a) Architecture & Ecology
b) Archaeology & Ecology
c) Architecture & Palaeontology
d) Archaeology & Palaeontology

5. Which country is well known for its artificial islands?

a) China
b) Dubai
c) France
d) USA

6. Which of the following architects works mostly with naturally grown buildings?

a) Mitchel Joachim
b) Pamela Warhust
c) Michael Pawlyn
d) Dan Philips

7. The project known as the 'high line' built a park on top of which of the following?

a) A skyscraper
b) An old residence building
c) A hill
d) An old set of train track

8. The Lowline park, is a postponed park project in NYC. What was significant about it?

a) It was underground
b) It contained no plants
c) It was a hoax
d) It was a cannabis plantation

9. The concept of breathable exteriors, developed by Doris Kim Sung, have which main aim?

a) Natural lighting
b) Energy-efficiency
c) Water conservation
d) Cladding

10. What is the name given to organically grown buildings that slowly attract carbon from the surrounding environment and become protected by a shell of calcium carbonate over time?

a) saccharomyces cerevisiae
b) coccolithophore
c) amoeba proteus
d) euglena virdis

091
ARCHITECTURE IN DUBAI

1. What is the architectural style of the Burj Khalifa skyscraper?

a) Neo-futurism
b) High-tech
c) Interactive
d) Hostile

2. Which of these famous building has starred in Hollywood blockbusters, such as 'Mission: Impossible – Ghost Protocol,' and 'Syriana'?

a) Burj Khalifa
b) The Opus
c) Burj al Arab
d) The Green Planet

3. Which building was the first and only foray into Dubai for the legendary late architect Zaha Hadid?

a) Burj Khalifa
b) The Opus
c) Burj al Arab
d) The Green Planet

4. The Cayan Tower's majestic helical design was achieved by rotating each floor how many degrees clockwise, so that the tower twists a full 90 degrees?

a) 1
b) 1.2
c) 1.4
d) 1.6

5. In which year did the Dubai Frame open?

a) 2016
b) 2017
c) 2018
d) 2019

6. Which material is the Gevora Hotel façade made of?

a) Gold
b) Glass
c) Steel
d) Concrete

7. How many stories high is The Green Planet?

a) 4
b) 14
c) 24
d) 34

8. The Atlantis Palm resort has two accommodation wings, consisting of the East and the West Tower, linked together by which suite?

a) The Arabic Bridge Suite
b) The Maritime Bridge Suite
c) The Atlantic Bridge Suite
d) The Royal Bridge Suite

9. Beyond the arrival zone in Five Palm Jumeirah Dubai lies a swimming pool. How long is it?

a) 30m (98ft)
b) 50m (164ft)
c) 60m (197ft)
d) 70m (230ft)

10. The Museum of the Future will be inscribed with Arabic calligraphy, and will act as an incubator for what?

a) Industry
b) Innovation
c) Science
d) Mathematics

092
AUSTRALIAN ARCHITECTURE

1. Which of these is considered to be one of the 20th century's most iconic buildings and definitely Australia's most famous building?

a) The Royal Exhibiton Building
b) Eureka Tower
c) Parliament House
d) Sydney Opera House

2. Which clock tower is the design of Brisbane City Hall clock tower based upon?

a) St.Mark's Campanile, Venice
b) Big Ben, London
c) Makkah Royal Clock Tower, Mecca
d) Astronomical Clock, Prague

3. Which of these buildings became the first in Australia to be awarded UNESCO World Heritage status?

a) Brisbane City Hall
b) The Royal Exhibition Building
c) Sydney Opera House
d) Port Arthur Historic Site

4. Australian Convict Sites is a World Heritage property consisting of how many remnant penal sites originally built during the 18th and 19th centuries?

a) 8
b) 9
c) 10
d) 11

5. Which of these is not a Australian architect?

a) Robin Boyd
b) Lily Isabel Maude Addison
c) Álvaro Joaquim de Melo Siza
d) Walter Liberty Vernon

6. Which is the tallest building in Australia, at 322.5m high?

a) Q1 Tower
b) Brisbane Skytower
c) 101 Collins street
d) Rialto Towers

7. How many conjoined towers does Rialto Towers, Melbourne comprise of?

a) 1
b) 2
c) 3
d) 4

8. Which of these buildings is considered as "a postmodern building that pays homage to New York's most famous art deco buildings, the Empire State Building and the Chrysler Building"?

a) Q1 Tower
b) Infinity Tower
c) Eureka Tower
d) 120 Collins Street

9. Which architectural style would you find at Queen Victoria Building in Sydney?

a) Romanesque Revival
b) Gothic
c) Mediterranean Revival
d) Post modern

10. Where is Australia Square Tower located?

a) Brisbane
b) Sydney
c) Canberra
d) Melbourne

093

WHERE ARE THESE BUILDINGS LOCATED?

1. Independence Temple

a) Missouri, U.S
b) India
c) Japan
d) Florida, U.S

2. Ren Building

a) Germany
b) France
c) China
d) Canada

3. Zayed National Museum

a) Iran
b) United Arab Emirates
c) Russia
d) Iraq

4. Basket Building

a) Mississippi
b) Brazil
c) Chile
d) Ohio

5. The Church of Hallgrimur

a) Iceland
b) UK
c) France
d) Italy

6. Cybertecture Egg Office Building

a) Netherlands
b) China
c) India
d) Argentina

7. Bubble Palace

a) Switzerland
b) France
c) Germany
d) Belgium

8. Casa Terracota

a) Colombia
b) Brazil
c) Venezuela
d) Mexico

9. Cubic Houses

a) Greece
b) Montenegro
c) Albania
d) Netherlands

10. Sharp Center for Design

a) Sweden
b) Canada
c) Spain
d) U.S

094

ITALIAN ARCHITECTURE

1. What is the most important cathedral of the Italian renaissance and the largest church in the world?

a) St. Mark's Cathedral
b) St. Peter's Basilica
c) Florence Cathedral
d) St. Paul's Cathedral

2. What is the second largest palace in Italy, designed by Filippo Bruneleschi?

a) Palazzo Pitti
b) Palazzo Farnese
c) Palazzo Ricardi
d) Vatican Palace

3. What is the function of The Leaning Tower of Pisa?

a) An administrative building
b) A fortification
c) A watchtower
d) The city cathedral's bell tower

4. In which architectural style was the Milan Cathedral built?

a) Gothic
b) Neoclassical
c) Victorian
d) Ancient Roman Architecture

5. What is the oldest bridge in Florence?

a) Rialto Bridge
b) St. Trinity Bridge
c) Ponte Vecchio
d) Ponte alla Grazie

6. What is the shape of Castel Sant'Angelo in Rome?

a) Cylindrical
b) Conic
c) Pyramidal
d) Cubic

7. In Italian Baroque architecture, what does the word 'undulate' mean?

a) Flat with no definition or surface pattern
b) Wavy or appearing wave-like
c) Textured and patterned with rustic elements
d) Scroll-like or spiral forms

8. Who was the first Roman Renaissance architect to design the original Greek cross plan?

a) Carlo Maderna
b) Raphael
c) Michelangelo
d) Donato Bramante

9. Which architect proposed the Latin cross plan?

a) Carlo Maderna
b) Raphael
c) Michelangelo
d) Donato Bramante

10. What does "piano nobile" mean in Italian architecture?

a) Internal court surrounded by an arcade
b) A method of forming a stone work with roughened surface
c) Several steps going up, 3 steps going down
d) The last floor of a palace

095
ARCHITECTURAL TERMS

1. What is an arris?

a) The highest point of a roof
b) A protective covering
c) The sharp edge formed by the intersection of two surfaces
d) A manner of tiling

2. What is a balconette?

a) A very large balcony
b) A false balcony
c) An internal balcony
d) A glass balcony

3. What is another name for a technical, scale drawing of something?

a) Red copy
b) Black plan
c) White print
d) Blueprint

4. Cantilever, suspension and swing are all types of what common construction?

a) Skyscraper
b) Bridge
c) Monument
d) Church

5. Which of these is not a sort of decorative moulding?

a) Inglenook
b) Vitruvian scroll
c) Egg-and-dart
d) Anthemion

Answers to 094

1. b) St. Peter's Basilica
2. a) Palazzo Pitti
3. d) The city cathedral's bell tower
4. a) Gothic
5. c) Ponte Vechio
6. a) Cylindrical
7. b) Wavy or appearing wave-like
8. d) Donato Bramante
9. b) Raphael
10. c) Several steps going up, 3 steps going down

6. What name is given to a row of columns that are spaced consistently and connected above by a horizontal entablature?

a) Casement
b) Buttress
c) Colonnade
d) Cornice

7. A portico is a porch leading to the entrance of a building, what are they usually supported by?

a) Rafters
b) Columns
c) Lintels
d) Parapets

8. What name is given to an architectural structure built against or projecting from a wall which serves to support or reinforce the wall?

a) Column
b) Beam
c) Pole
d) Buttress

9. Which of these is not a style of roof?

a) Lucarne
b) Gabel
c) Mansard
d) Gambrel

10. What is a plinth?

a) A horizontal beam over a door or window
b) A tall, ornamental post at the landing of a staircase
c) A block on which a pedestal, column, or statue is placed
d) A strip of wood or metal which separates panes of glass in a window

096
SCANDINAVIAN ARCHITECTURE

1. Scandinavian interior design is characterized by which of the following?

a) Simplicity
b) Functionality
c) Minimalism
d) All of them

2. Who is considered to be the most famous Scandinavian architect?

a) Rem Koolhaas
b) Jean Nouvel
c) Bjarke Ingels
d) Daniel Libeskind

3. Which of these is a feature of Scandinavian architecture?

a) Natural light
b) Sleek shapes
c) Energy efficiency
d) All of them

4. What is the most prestigious architectural distinction in Scandinavia?

a) Nykredit Architecture Award
b) Alvar Aalto Medal
c) AIA Gold Medal
d) The AR House Awards

5. In which architectural style is Stokholm City Hall building built?

a) Brutalist
b) Deconstructivist
c) Art Nouveau
d) Neoclassic

6. Which of these Nordic architects has been awarded Pritzker Prize?

a) Arne Jacobsen
b) Sverre Fehn
c) Bjarke Ingels
d) all of them

7. Who was the architect of Helsinki Central Station?

a) Eliel Saarinen
b) Martin Nyrop
c) Ferdinand Meldahl
d) Vilhelm Wohlert

8. Oslo City Hall is built from which material?

a) Concrete
b) Wood
c) Steel and glass
d) Red bricks

9. How many towers does Oslo City Hall have?

a) 1
b) 2
c) 3
d) 4

10. What is the Tromsdalen church in Norway also known as?

a) The Arctic Cathedral
b) The Nordic Cathedral
c) The Swedish Cathedral
d) The Gateway to Heaven

097
FRANK LLOYD WRIGHT

1. Which architectural style did Frank Lloyd Wright develop?

a) Contemporary architecture
b) Colonial Revival
c) Prairie School
d) Bauhaus

2. Which of these buildings is not designed by Frank Lloyd Wright?

a) Walt Disney Concert Hall, California
b) Fallingwater, Mill Run, Pennsylvania
c) Taliesin West, Scottsdale, Arizona
d) The Guggenheim Museum, New York

3. Who did Frank Lloyd Wright work for in his early career?

a) Le Corbusier
b) Walter Gropius
c) Pierre Jeanneret
d) Louis Sullivan

4. Which of the following prizes were awarded to Frank Lloyd Wright?

a) The Twenty-five Year Award
b) AIA Gold Medal
c) Royal Gold Medal
d) All of them

5. How many buildings of Frank Lloyd Wright were designated as World Heritage Sites by UNESCO in 2019?

a) 4
b) 6
c) 8
d) 10

6. Which construction material did Frank Lloyd Wright mostly use?

a) Concrete
b) Bricks
c) Stone
d) Glass

7. What were some characteristics of Frank Lloyd Wright's style?

a) Overhanging eaves
b) Open floor plans
c) Both of them
d) None of them

8. Did Frank Lloyd Wright win the Pritzker prize?

a) Yes
b) No
c) He rejected it
d) He was awarded the prize after death

9. How many houses are known as textile block houses were built by Wright in the Los Angeles area?

a) 2
b) 3
c) 4
d) 5

10. In which year did Frank Lloyd Wright die?

a) 1959
b) 1965
c) 1970
d) 1973

098
WORLD FAMOUS TOWERS

1. What material is Galata Tower in Istanbul made of?

a) Stone
b) Bricks
c) Steel
d) Concrete

2. Where is the Minaret of Jam, built in the 12th century as part of a mosque, located?

a) Iraq
b) Afghanistan
c) Iran
d) India

3. When was Belem Tower, Lisbon built?

a) 16th century
b) 17th century
c) 18th century
d) 19th century

4. What is considered as the world's tallest brick minaret, with a total height of 72m (236ft)?

a) Spiral Minaret
b) Minaret of Jam
c) Kutlug Timur Minaret
d) Qutb Minar

5. Which of The Three Pagodas in China is taller and older?

a) The left pagoda
b) The middle pagoda
c) The right pagoda
d) They are exactly the same

1. c) Prairie School
2. a) Walt Disney Concert Hall, California
3. d) Louis Sullivan
4. d) All of them
5. c) 8
6. a) Concrete
7. c) Both of them
8. b) No
9. c) 4
10. a) 1959

6. The CN Tower is one of the most recognizable icons of which country?

a) U.S
b) China
c) Canada
d) United Arab Emirates

7. Nicknamed the medieval Manhattan, San Gimignano is a village in Tuscany famous for its stone towers. How many does it have?

a) 11
b) 12
c) 13
d) 14

8. The name Big Ben refers to which part of the London landmark?

a) The clock tower
b) The bell which is housed in the tower
c) Both of them
d) None of them

9. How many metres high is the King Ezana's Stela, which is actually the tallest standing tower in the ancient city of Axum, Ethiopia?

a) 24m (79ft)
b) 34m (112ft)
c) 44m (144ft)
d) 54m (177ft)

10. How many steps does the Italian Tower of Pisa have?

a) 256
b) 276
c) 296
d) 316

099
CHINESE ARCHITECTURE #2

1. Ancient Chinese architecture mainly used which materials?

a) Bricks & stones
b) Timber
c) Clay & sand
d) All of them

2. How many different roof types would you find in Chinese architecture?

a) 1
b) 2
c) 3
d) 4

3. What is the oldest known surviving stone construction in China, built during the Sui Dynasty (AD 581-618)?

a) Zhaozhou Bridge
b) Great Wall of China
c) Luoyang Bridge
d) Portala Palace

4. How tall is the Songyue Pagoda, the earliest known brick pagoda in China?

a) 20m (66ft)
b) 40m (131ft)
c) 60m (197ft)
d) 80m (262ft)

5. Approximately how old is the Great Wall of China?

a) 2000 years
b) 2300 years
c) 2600 years
d) 2900 years

6. Which cities in China does the Grand Canal link?

a) Beijing and Hangzhou
b) Beijing and Wuhan
c) Shanghai and Shenzhen
d) Shanghai and Tianjin

7. How many years did it take to finish the Leshan Giant Buddha?

a) 60
b) 70
c) 80
d) 90

8. The Forbidden City was the Imperial palace of which dynasties?

a) Zhou and Qin
b) Sui and Tang
c) Ming and Qing
d) None of them

9. The Potala Palace is considered a model of which architectural style?

a) Taoist architecture
b) Shinto architecture
c) Tibetan architecture
d) Buddhist architecture

10. Which of these Chinese architects have won the Pritzker prize?

a) I. M. Pei
b) Wang Shu
c) None of them
d) Both of them

100
PARISIAN ARCHITECTURE

Answers on p.9

1. Paris is the birthplace of which architectural style?

a) Gothic
b) Baroque
c) De Stijl
d) Brutalist

2. Who was the lead architect of Center Georges Pompidou?

a) Frank Gehry
b) Rem Koolhaas
c) Norman Foster
d) Renzo Piano

3. How tall is the Eiffel Tower?

a) 298m (978ft)
b) 324m (1063ft)
c) 356m (1168ft)
d) 400m (1312ft)

4. The Pyramid of the Louvre is built in the same proportions as which famous pyramid?

a) Pyramid of Khafre
b) Pyramid of Djoser
c) Pyramid of Giza
d) Pyramid of Menkaure

5. Which of these villas were designed by Le Corbusier?

a) Ville La Roche
b) Ville Jeanneret
c) Ville Savoie
d) all of them

6. What is situated on the top of Montmartre Hill?

a) Basilique de Sacre-Coeur
b) Moulin Rouge
c) The Museum of Modern Art
d) McDonalds

7. What was added to the facade of the Notre-Dame de Paris in about 1240?

a) Gargoyles
b) Dragons
c) Gnomes
d) Faries

8. Which square is the symbol of freedom for the French people?

a) The Dauphine Square
b) Place de la Concorde
c) Place de la Bastille
d) The Victory Square

9. How many bridges does the city of Paris have?

a) 25
b) 37
c) 42
d) 59

10. Arc de Triomphe is placed at the center of Place de l'Étoile—the étoile or "star" is formed by the juncture of how many radiating avenues?

a) 5
b) 8
c) 9
d) 12